4585

God's Everlasting "Yes"

AND OTHER SERMONS

God's Everlasting "Yes"

AND OTHER SERMONS

Ilion T. Jones

WORD BOOKS

Waco, Texas  London, England

Preface

For fifty years now I have had a special interest in preaching, roughly two-thirds of that time as a preacher and one-third as a teacher of preaching. Because of my special interest in this field I have in recent years become keenly and sometimes painfully aware of what many observers agree is a distinct decline in the importance of preaching and in its quality within Protestantism.

A common current complaint about preaching is that preachers no longer talk in biblical language, but rather in the language of technical theologians, philosophers, sociologists, semanticists, and the like. Those who make this complaint invariably go on to say that preachers might as well be talking in a foreign language for all the practical help they offer the hearers.

So, I have reluctantly come to the conclusion that entirely too large a proportion of Protestant preachers seem not to be interested in using the Bible as the basis of their sermons, or else do not know how to handle texts and passages of Scripture in their sermonizing. Specifically, they seem not to know how to utilize the several available types of sermon structures to develop a biblical truth, how to find and make use of suitable supporting illustrative material, and how to help laymen better to understand our basic Christian doctrines and put them to work in their daily lives. In short, our ministers are not only neglecting preaching itself but neglecting many of the fundamental principles of effective preaching that we teachers in this field call the "techniques" of sermonizing.

I have, therefore, undertaken to prepare a few of my recent sermons for publication, hoping that those ministers who once sat in my classes, those who have read and studied my textbook on preaching, and those who preach regularly week by week, may find in these sermons some helpful suggestions as to how to find a truth in some portion of the Scriptures and to structure a sermon that develops it, how to unfold and illustrate it, and how to apply it to the problems of ordinary people.

I hope also that some laymen will be interested in reading them to discover new light on the relevance of the Bible and of our Christian doctrines to their daily lives and that all readers will find them spiritually helpful.

ILION T. JONES

Contents

GOD'S EVERLASTING "YES"

For the Son of God, Jesus Christ, whom we preached among you,
Silvanus and Timothy and I, was not Yes and No; but in him it is
always Yes. For all the promises of God find their Yes in him. That
is why we utter the Amen through him, to the glory of God.

—II CORINTHIANS 1:19-20

I

ONE WHO STUDIES the letters of Paul soon becomes
impressed with the casual, unexpected manner in which
Paul sets forth some of his daring, sublime truths about our Christian Gospel. An illustration of this is found in the first chapter of
his second letter to the Corinthians.

He had promised to visit the church at Corinth and had been
forced by circumstances beyond his control, seemingly more
than once, to change his plans. Some people in the church were
charging him with vacillating, with being fickle, or even capricious, with saying now "yes" and then "no" without taking his
words seriously. He refers to the charge, denies it, and then says,
in effect, "Call my promises vacillation if you wish, but the
Gospel of Christ we preach is not something now 'yes' and then
'no.' *In him it is always yes!* All the promises of God find their
'yes' in Christ." This is one way of saying that Christ is God's
clear-cut, positive answer to all our human questions, to all our
human needs, to all our human hopes and dreams. Or, to borrow
an expression from Thomas Carlyle, the noted English essayist,
Christ is God's "Everlasting Yes."

9

Then Paul adds, "That is why we utter the Amen through him to the glory of God." The word "Amen" was used by Paul in a different meaning from the way we ordinarily use it. That word to us has come to mean the way to conclude a public prayer, as if the leader is saying, "That concludes what I have to say." Originally it was not the leader of the prayer who used it, but the people who were present. They used it in its literal meaning of "So be it," meaning, "We join in, subscribe to that prayer," or "You have expressed our petitions." Later, but just when is not definitely known, the people came also to say "Amen" to what the preacher was saying. When I was a boy I often heard "Amens" from the congregations while the minister was preaching or praying. Those "Amens" signified that the listeners agreed with, wholeheartedly supported, and solemnly ratified what was being proclaimed in the sermon or said in the prayer. In recent years congregations are being taught to use what we call the "People's Amen" at the conclusion of the leader's prayers.

Hence, when Paul said, "We utter the Amen through Christ to the glory of God," he was really saying, "We believe in, joyfully accept, and loyally support the Gospel. We propose to live by it. We dedicate ourselves to its proclamation. In short, to God's yes, God's affirmations in Christ, we give our resounding human yes, our affirmations, our Amens." That, or something like that, is what every Christian's public profession of faith in Christ ought to signify. The question is: Have we really said Amen to Christ in that sense, to that degree? Have we ratified the Gospel with enthusiasm, with "our lives, our fortunes, and our sacred honor"?

II

1. The values of negations.

The first thing that should be said is that negations have their values. They serve useful functions. The word "no" has its proper place in the Christian's vocabulary. Jesus said no to many practices and beliefs and encouraged his followers to do likewise.

He made it crystal clear what he believed and what he did not believe, though he went beyond the "Thou shalt nots" of the old Jewish law. The early Christians also said no to many practices and beliefs of their times. William James, the Harvard philosopher, was right when he declared that every person needs some "No! No!" in his character to make him strong.

When someone asked Mr. Einstein how he came to discover the theory of relativity he said, "By challenging an axiom." Now and then a belief commonly accepted as axiomatic must be challenged or even rejected in order to clear the way for the discovery of truth. Under certain conditions negations may be a form of knowledge. After a long period of time in which Mr. Edison and his laboratory assistants had performed 699 experiments without finding what they were searching for, one assistant exclaimed in disgust, "699 experiments and we have learned nothing." Mr. Edison replied, "Oh, yes, we have learned something. We have learned 699 things that will not work." And, according to the report, on their 700th effort they succeeded. It is of tremendous importance to the human race to discover the things that will not—that cannot—work in this world.

But every negation should have in view an ultimate affirmation. We ask questions to find answers. We deny falsehoods because we are looking for the truth. We reject the wrong way of life because we are searching for the right way. We can judge something to be untrue or unwholesome because we can compare it with what we know or believe to be true and wholesome. Michelangelo, the great artist, said, "I criticise by creating." We should criticise the unchristian way of life by demonstrating the superior worth of the genuine Christian way. That is to say, the function of negation is definitely limited in its scope. It is not an end in itself but a means to something beyond and better than itself.

Tennyson once claimed, "There is more faith in honest doubt than in half our creeds." And there is, provided—*provided* one does what Tennyson did, wrestles with doubt with the determination to resolve it and to arrive at a faith to accept and live by. Tennyson's poem *In Memoriam* is evidence of that. *In Memoriam* is not one poem but a collection of 131 separate poems written over a period of three years or more. These poems, each of which is easily dated, record the doubts and agonies through which the poet passed on his way to faith. When he had found faith, he wrote another poem and made it a prologue to all the others, which he then put together in chronological order, entitling them *In Memoriam*. He summarized his faith somewhat in these lines:

> Strong Son of God, immortal Love,
>   Whom we, that have not seen thy face.
>   By faith, and faith alone, embrace,
> Believing where we cannot prove;
>
> . . . .
>
> Thou seemest human and divine,
>   The highest, holiest manhood, thou.
>   Our wills are ours, we know not how;
> Our wills are ours, to make them thine.

Make note of the fact that when he found a faith he dedicated himself to it with all of his heart.

2. The dangers and limitations of negations.

It is possible for one to become an expert at pointing out errors in the thinking of others and still have a sterile mind of his own. A person can reject one error after another without engendering any enthusiasm for positive truths or even feeling any responsibility for doing so. One of the world's well-known critics of Christianity was the French philosopher Voltaire, who died about 1778. He played a prominent part in producing the skepticism and the anti-religion of the late 18th and early 19th centuries. About the middle of the 19th century, when a return to faith and a revival of religion began to appear in Europe and the United States, Thomas Carlyle, the English essayist mentioned earlier, in a famous apostrophe to the deceased Voltaire said something like this: "Your appointed task is finished. You

have made your case that we cannot teach the Christian religion
in the 18th century as it was taught in the 8th century. What
next? Will you help us to embody the divine Spirit of that religion in a new vehicle and vesture, that our souls may live?
What? You have no faculty in that kind? Only a torch for burn-
ing, no hammer for building? Take our thanks, then, and take
yourself away." Then to his readers, many of whom manifestly
were professing Christians and Christian ministers, he literally
shouted: "Produce! Were it but the pitifullest infinitesimal
fraction of a product. Produce it in God's name!" We can produce the fruits of a noble life only by launching out on what
we believe, not by trying to live on what we deny; on what we
accept, not on what we reject.

James Russell Lowell once described a person thus:

A brain she has that never errs,
And yet is never nobly right;
It does not leap to great results
But in some corner out of sight
Suspects a spot of latent blight
And o'er the impatient infinite
She bargains, haggles and consults.

The creative work of the world is accomplished only by those
who are "nobly right," whose minds "leap to great results," who
explore the potentialities of their major affirmations.

The Apostle Paul spoke of those who "listen to anybody and
can never arrive at a knowledge of the truth" (II Tim. 3:7),
and those who are "tossed to and fro and carried about with
every wind of doctrine" (Eph. 4:14). People without guidelines for their lives, without positive convictions and beliefs of
their own, are always at sea and consequently never find the full
meanings of life. They are like the janitor of a church of whom
I heard recently. When asked how he managed to get along
with so many men and women telling him what to do, he replied, "Well, I just throw my mind into neutral and go where
I am pushed." But a person who has a positive purpose or con-

viction to guide him can always push his way ahead. A missionary
in a concentration camp in Japan during the last war said she
was sustained those years by the old saying, "All the darkness
in the world cannot put out the light of a single candle." Her
faith in Christ never dimmed. Did not Christ say: "I am the
light of the world; he who follows me will not walk in darkness,
but will have the light of life" (John 8:12). *A Light. A Way. An
Open Door Ahead!*

3. *The necessity of affirmations.*

Many of us Christians overlook these limitations and dangers
of negations. We have changed Paul's assertion, "In Christ it is
always 'Yes,' " to "In Christ it is always 'No.' " With pride we
declare, "As a Christian here are the things I will not and cannot
believe, or subscribe to, or approve of, or do." But too seldom
we say, "Here is what I believe, subscribe to, approve of, and
practice." In short, we forget that it is impossible for us to live
creatively by our negations. We can live creatively only by
launching out on our affirmations.

It is not possible to build a strong, wholesome personality on
negations. The most vulnerable person in the world, morally
speaking, is one whose moral code consists solely of things he will
not do. Someone has said that one of the mean types of characters
is the "cowardly virtuous person who never does wrong because
he is afraid to, but who is never in love with the right, never
affirms the right positively." That person is already spiritually
dying who tries to live by his disgusts instead of by his admira-
tions, by the things he is angry at or hates instead of by the things
he loves.

We cannot build durable friendships and marriages on negations. Have you heard of the person who said, "I guess you would
call us friends: we have the same enemies?" A character in fiction
whose marriage ended in divorce said, on the day his divorce
became final, "Our shared doubts have been the only things we
had in common. They are not enough." Indeed, they are not
enough! A successful marriage is formed out of shared interests

and tastes, shared hopes and dreams, shared convictions and ideals.

We cannot build a strong country on negations. George Santayana, the philosopher and novelist, once said that the hollowness of his father's liberal politics began to dawn upon him one day, when his father was expressing himself vehemently about things he did not like. He asked him, "What ideal society would you approve, Father?" His father replied, "I don't know what I want, but I know what I don't want." Historians tell us that the trouble with most all revolutions is that their supporters have a clear notion of what they hate, what they mean to destroy; but dim, cloudy notions of what they want to create. For that reason most revolutionary movements are destructive instead of constructive. If we expect to build an enduring free society in this America of ours we citizens must have a passionate faith in the democratic way of life, a clear notion of what that way of life involves and a never-lagging zeal to support these with all our human resources.

We cannot build a wholesome, fruitful spiritual life on negations. Professor John Erskine of Columbia University used to say to his classes, and undoubtedly provoked a chuckle each time he said it, "Most people have some sort of religion. At least they know what church they are staying away from." That doesn't qualify as a religion in any sense of the word. A true religion must have positive content. It consists of beliefs that are put to work creatively in one's life and relations. Otherwise it is a misnomer.

We need to put positive beliefs into practical living, to take firm hold of great affirmations and follow where they lead, if we wish to get the most and the best out of life as God intended us to.

4. Christianity is a religion of positives.

In spite of all that you have heard to the contrary, Christianity is and always has been essentially a religion of positives. Jesus said, "I am the way and the truth and the life" (John

14: 16). No Christian will ever know what life can be for him until he believes that and launches out on his belief without hesitation, even with a certain degree of abandon. The psalmist challenged his readers to "taste and see that the Lord is good" (Psalm 34:8), that is, to put religion to the test of experience. Jesus declared, "If any man's will is to do His will, he shall know whether the teaching is from God" (John 7:17). There is only one way to discover the values of Christian faith, and that is to put it to work, to practice it, to live by it.

One reason for the weakness of the church and of Christians is that we have not said "Amen" to Christ in the full sense of that word as it was used by the Apostle Paul. I ask you, have you really said "yes" to all the truths of the Gospel? Have you tried them out in your life? Have you planted them in your soul and given them a chance to take root and spring to life and bear fruit?

A pilot on a Mississippi riverboat who had been on that job for thirty-five years was asked, "I suppose you know where all the rocks and sandbanks are?" He replied, "No, but I know where the deep water is." Sadly enough, far too many of us Christians seem more concerned about what to avoid than about what to do, about where not to go than about where to go, to find the fullness of life in Christ.

Over the years, I have many times been in a position to observe the different ways in which Christians meet the crucial experiences of life. To some Christians their faith seems to make little difference in their life-situations, while to others it makes all the difference. To some their faith is an unimportant factor; to others, the determining factor in the outcome of life's crucial experiences.

The faith of some seems to be casual, formal, incidental, external—the observance of a custom which does not provide them with resources to meet and master misfortune, to conquer temptations, to generate enthusiasm and noble purpose with which to make their lives count effectually for Christ in their chosen places in society.

The faith of others seems to be a positive, vital, productive, dynamic, controlling factor in every situation. They really are aware of the presence and power of God. They have discovered what Jesus promised his followers they could and would find if they asked and sought and knocked, namely, the bread of life, the water of life, the power at work in them that would enable them to do far more abundantly than they could ask or think, or certainly more than they could possibly generate by themselves. Or to put it briefly, they really could say, "I know in whom I believe and am persuaded that He is real, and able to do what He promises." They really meant it when they said "Amen" to Christ.

III

Thomas Huxley, the well-known agnostic of the last century, the man who is credited with having coined the term "agnostic," who denied many beliefs commonly accepted by his contemporaries, because he seemed unwilling or unable to believe very few things, once said rather wistfully, "The longer I live the more obvious it is that the most sacred act of a man's life is to say, 'I believe such and such to be true.' " That *is* a sacred act, if a person says it with all his heart and backs it up with his deeds. Huxley seems to have discovered at long last that our souls subsist on what we believe, not on what we deny. The philosopher Spinoza rightfully claimed that a man really believes something when he acts as if it is true.

To return to where we began: When Paul told how the early Christians said "Amen" to all that God had revealed in Christ, he simply meant that they were saying "yes" to Christ, by acting as if it were true, by giving the Gospel a chance to prove itself in their lives and in their relations.

One of the best down-to-earth definitions of salvation I ever heard was that one given by Dr. William Adams Brown, an outstanding theologian of an older generation. He said, "To be saved is to be set free for the good." Do we—you and I—know what we have been saved *for* as well as what we have been saved *from?*

My message, succinctly stated, then is simply this: Don't go through life as a question mark, as a rebel, as an iconoclast, trying to live by your negations. Believe something! Live by your affirmations! Launch out on them with abandon, with zest and zeal. That is the only way to discover to its fullest possibilities the meaning, the wonder of our human life!

SUCCESSFUL FAILURE

I want you to know, brethren, that what has happened to me has really served to advance the gospel.

—PHILIPPIANS 1:12

I

A N ARTICLE in the science section of *Time* magazine some time ago was entitled "Successful Failure." It told about what was known as "Operation Echo A12." A Thor rocket was launched from Cape Kennedy with a tightly deflated balloon which was supposed to expand or inflate for the sole purpose of testing a new form of aluminized film that would stay rigid after the gas that blew up the balloon had escaped through meteor punctures. Things didn't go exactly as planned. But fortunately the TV pictures that were flashed back told the scientists what had gone wrong, so that they could avoid the same error again. The reporter headlined this as a "Successful Failure."

"Successful failure"! That is an expression worth meditating about. There are a number of successful failures mentioned in the Bible, one of which Paul tells about in the first chapter of his letter to the Philippians. Paul had planned after a trip through Macedonia and Achaia and then to Jerusalem, to go to Rome to preach the gospel (cf. Acts 19:21). He finally went to Rome, but not exactly as he had planned. He went as a prisoner. In Jerusalem he was mobbed, arrested, and imprisoned; he finally decided to appeal to Caesar for his trial. This made it necessary for him to be sent to Rome to be tried before the Emperor's tribunal. It looked as if his plans to preach the gospel in Rome, the very heart of the Empire, had failed ingloriously. After some time in Rome as a prisoner, he wrote to his friends at Philippi in Macedonia that his imprisonment had unexpectedly "turned out" to be a means of advancing his cause. He told them that the gospel had penetrated the whole Praetorian guard (probably through the soldiers to whom he was shackled, and to whom he conversed about the gospel), that the Christian brethren in Rome had been emboldened to preach the gospel with more vigor, and without fear, and that he himself was more hopeful of finally being acquitted. Hence, he said, they had all come to realize that even in this imprisonment Christ has been honored. In short, his experience was a successful failure. His whole letter to his friends was a prayer of thanksgiving to God for providentially overruling his misfortune for the good of himself and of his fellow workers and for the spread of the gospel.

II

In our lifetime most of us have a variety of experiences that seem to be failures: failures to succeed at an important undertaking, to realize hopes and dreams, to live up to our intentions and resolutions, to become our best selves; failures to make a success of our human relations, to overcome temptations; failures of attitude, of disposition; moral and ethical failures. But nothing—not even our gravest sin—is a failure, if . . . . Ah! that "if" is a large one, tremendously important, fraught with divine destiny.

1. An experience is not a failure if it prods us to keep on trying.

What if scientists had given up when they failed? The world would have been much poorer and progress much slower if they

had done this. Thomas A. Edison and his associates once performed nearly a thousand experiments before they finally succeeded in what they were attempting to achieve. It would be
interesting to know how many efforts of our scientists to explore
outer space have been failures up to now. Suppose Winston
Churchill had quit when he had been repudiated by his countrymen? The world would have lost the services of one of its outstanding statesmen. What if Peter had quit when he denied
Jesus, or Paul had quit when he was sent to prison, or our Lord
had quit when they drove him out of the synagogue at the beginning of his earthly ministry? Where would Christianity be
now? What kind of a society would we have now if our parents,
our school teachers, our leaders in every field of human endeavor
and hosts of ordinary folk in our world had quit when they were
not succeeding in their efforts?

Very few people accomplish anything worthwhile the first
time they attempt it. In fact, very few people's careers consist of
continuous successes and no failures.

> Heaven is not reached at a single bound;
> But we build the ladder by which we rise
> From the lowly earth to the vaulted skies,
> And we mount to its summit round by round.
> JOSIAH G. HOLLAND

Failures are a test of our mettle. They are a challenge to keep
on trying. They awaken the soul's courage. Emerson said:
"Failure is endeavor and endeavor persisted in is never failure."
Edward Arlington Robinson, the poet, has this line in one of his
poems: "I haven't failed: I've merely not achieved."

I remind you that one of the basic tenets of our Judaic-Chris-
tian faith is that God doesn't get discouraged and therefore we
should not. One of the noblest utterances in any religious literature is what Isaiah said to his people, who were in exile in a
foreign land and who had all but lost heart and given up hope of
any future as a people. He called them the servant of God and
in God's name said, "Behold my servant whom I uphold, my

chosen, in whom my soul delights; I have put my spirit upon him. . . . He will not fail or be discouraged till he has established justice in the earth . . ." (Isaiah 42:1,4). The implication of this is, "Therefore, do not lose heart, or quit, in the fight of life." So Paul said to the Christians: "And let us not grow weary in well-doing, for in due season we shall reap, if we do not lose heart" (Gal. 6:9).

2. An experience is not a failure if through it we discover why we failed and put that knowledge to good use.

In one of his letters, D. H. Lawrence wrote, "If only we could have two lives, the first in which to make one's mistakes, which seem as if they have to be made, and the second to profit by them." Fortunately we don't have to wait for a second chance at living to profit by our mistakes. "A man who has committed a mistake, and does not correct it, is committing another mistake." Similarly, a person who fails and doesn't figure out why and profit by it, has failed again. I think there is no doubt that all of us who have lived a few decades would agree that there is no greater guide to success than the lessons taught by our failures and mistakes.

Mr. Watson, the president of International Business Machines, is reported recently to have said to a discouraged young writer, "Every one of your rejected manuscripts was rejected for a reason. Have you pulled them to pieces looking for that reason? . . . You've got to put failure to work for you."

One of the best examples of a young man who put failure to work for him that I know of is found in the New Testament. I refer to the story of John Mark. He started out as the traveling companion and assistant of Barnabas and Paul on their first novel experience as itinerant missionaries. It was a long, hazardous undertaking. Mark stayed with them on the first lap of the journey through the island of Cyprus. But when they landed on the mainland of Asia Minor, he left them and returned to the security of his home in Jerusalem (Acts 13:13). Some years later when Paul and Barnabas were planning a second journey, Barnabas wished to take Mark along again. But Paul would not consent to this because he felt that Mark had failed them on the first journey. There was such a sharp difference of opinion between Paul and Barnabas that Barnabas took Mark and went one way, and Paul took Silas and went another way (Acts 15: 36ff). Many years thereafter when Paul was writing to his young associate Timothy, he said, "Get Mark and bring him with you, for he is very useful in serving me" (II Tim. 4:11). In the intervening years something had happened that is not known. But a man whom Paul once regarded as a quitter was finally recognized as a valuable helper. The last chapter in this man's life was this: he wrote the earliest and one of the most valuable of the four Gospels. That is a monument to the man who made good after a dismal failure. And I cannot help but believe that he probably made good because of his failure, because he figured out how and why he had failed and put his knowledge to good use.

Again I remind you of another doctrine of our Christian faith: the doctrine of repentance. The word "repentance" means literally turning around and going in the opposite direction: a complete reversal of our lives. When we fail, morally recognize the failure for what it is, figure out what caused it, and then decide to reorganize our lives on a different basis, we have repented. When Paul was making his defense before King Agrippa he told of preaching a gospel in which he called men to ". . . repent and turn to God and perform deeds worthy of their repentance" (Acts 26:20). If our repentance is genuine it will result in another kind of living. If our moral failures lead to genuine repentance, result in discovering why we failed and in beginning a new life, they are not failures.

We often say that there is nothing we can do about our past sins: what is written is written. But there *is* something very important that we can do about them. We can learn their lessons and put those lessons to work in nobler living. In so doing we at least ensure that our sins will not be wasted. We speak of God "redeeming" our sins. That word "redeem" is another meaningful word. It literally means release, receipt of ransom, liberation, setting free. It is not only release from sin but release to another type of life.

> Nor deem the irrevocable Past
> As wholly wasted, wholly vain,
> If rising on its wrecks at last
> To something higher we attain.
> HENRY WADSWORTH LONGFELLOW

3. An experience is not a failure if through it we discover our true selves.

One who reads biographies soon becomes impressed with two things: (1) Some of the most successful people in the world started out as failures. (2) Because they failed, they found themselves and their life's work. One comes to expect the stories of most great men's lives to follow that pattern.

When Nathaniel Hawthorne lost his position in the Custom House at Salem, Massachusetts, he came home utterly defeated to tell his wife that he was a complete failure. To his amazement she greeted his dismal news with delight, saying, "Now you can write your book." So he sat down and wrote *The Scarlet Letter,* still considered by many critics as the greatest novel ever written in our country. Whistler failed at West Point. After he was dropped from the list of students there, he halfheartedly tried engineering. Finally he tried painting, with the success that is well known. Phillips Brooks, the noted Episcopal minister who died in the 1890's, had planned to be a teacher and had prepared himself for the profession of teaching. But he failed so ingloriously that he became despondent. Then he prepared himself for the ministry. In this calling he made a huge success. A great many people in every generation are unhappy failures, for no other reason than that they have not found themselves, found out who they are and what they are fitted for. And if because of failure a person finally discovers where and how he can best use his talents for God, his failure must be regarded a success.

That is true also of our moral failures. In the parable of the prodigal son Jesus said that the older son living riotously in a far country "came to himself." This could have the unworthy meaning of the older son's simply having become so tired of such a life that he wanted a change. Or it could have the higher meaning of his having found out something significant about himself. Jesus surely intended to convey the latter meaning. The man discovered that he was not meant for that sort of life, that in his dissipation he was not his true self. When he "came to himself" he realized that he had a higher, divine destiny as a human being. This parable of Jesus is one of many passages on which another biblical doctrine is based: the doctrine of man, that man is made in the image of God and destined to live as becomes a child of God; that he is not intended to waste his manhood in loose, sinful, animalistic living.

It is not enough to regret the moral predicaments in which we find ourselves entangled because of our sin. We are on the way to redemption when we recognize that we have missed our calling, lost our way; when we decide we have a higher calling and get started on the right track.

> Defeat may serve as well as victory
> To shake the soul and let the glory out.
> EDWIN MARKHAM

4. An experience is not a failure if through it we become better disciplined personalities.

We moderns are afraid of that word *discipline*. But it is written large in our New Testament. We are cautioned by Peter: "Do not be surprised at the fiery ordeal which comes upon you to prove you, as though something strange were happening to you," but to "rejoice in so far as you share Christ's suffering" (I Pet. 4:12). And the writer of Hebrews tells us that "the Lord disciplines him whom he loves" (Heb. 12:6). Struggle and discipline are woven into the fabric of our lives in this world. Now Paul compares life to a foot race between well-trained athletes (I Cor.

9:24f; cf. also Heb. 12:1f) and now he compares it to a fight on a battlefield with the weapons of war (Eph. 6).

The person who faces the struggle with courage, meets it bravely with faith in the goodness, wisdom and love of God, and with implicit confidence that the God of all grace will undergird him and strengthen him and cause his discipline to yield "the peaceful fruits of righteousness" (1 Pet. 5:10; cf. Heb. 12:11)—that man will find himself a better person and will come to praise God for the privilege of sharing the sufferings of Christ. In brief compass this is our New Testament doctrine of discipline.

If our experiences, however bitter, however unfortunate, mellow our hearts, humble our spirits, purify our motives, cleanse our souls, make us more sensitive to spiritual values, more sympathetic toward our blundering human race—in short, if we take our so-called failures as instruments for the disciplining of our inner spirits—they are not failures, but successes, and, given time, they certainly will deserve to be called blessed.

> I call no fight a losing fight
> If, fighting, I have gained some straight new strength.
> If, fighting, I turned ever toward the light,
> All unallied with forces of the night.
>
> MIRIAM TEICHNER

5. An experience is not a failure if through it we come to a deeper faith in God.

This underlies, or is implied in, everything that has already been said. In one of his books Dr. Harry Emerson Fosdick tells of having a critical nervous breakdown in his young manhood. He said it was the most terrifying wilderness he ever traveled through, that he dreadfully wanted to commit suicide, but that instead he made some of the most vital discoveries of his life. That breakdown was the cause of his writing his priceless little book *The Meaning of Prayer*. One of the important discoveries he made was to find a real, vital belief in God, and that is the most important discovery that any person can make for his life.

In his letter to the Philippians Paul states that through the varied experiences of life—times of plenty and of want, times of sorrow and of joy, in any and all circumstances—he learned a great secret. That secret was to trust God, to leave everything in His hands, to be content—which, incidentally, literally means to become independent of outward circumstances. So he declared, "I can do all things in him who strengthens me" (Phil. 4:11-13).

That faith is the source of the morale that has so consistently characterized Christians throughout the centuries. That word "morale" is a great word. It means a state of psychological (mental, emotional) well-being, a sense of direction, confidence in the future. Whoever has this morale can take anything, go through anything without breaking down or giving up. This healthy state of mind is a blessed fruitage of faith in God. Karle Wilson Baker says, "Courage is fear that has said its prayers." The courageous British could call 1942 "nineteen fortitude" because they had said their prayers. I tell you there is no such thing as ultimate failure to a person who believes that a wise, all-powerful, loving, redeeming, regenerating, resurrecting God is in charge of this world and everything in it, and who makes that belief his working faith.

III

Dr. Ralph W. Sockman, who spent the whole of his ministry in one pastorate in New York City and who recently retired, tells of a public speaker who was conducting a forum in an Eastern city being asked by a person in the audience, "How can you say that there is a trustworthy Divine Administrator who guarantees the permanence of spiritual values when a character like Jesus suffered defeat?" The speaker thought a moment, looked the questioner straight in the eyes, and replied, "In the light of what Jesus accomplished during his days on the earth and in the centuries since, do you really think Jesus was defeated? No! he was a winning loser."

There you have it in a nutshell! No matter how much it appears that we have failed, we need not despair if the grace of God finds its way into the citadel of our souls to do these things for us and in us: to inspire us to keep on trying; to show us why we have failed; to make clear to us what we are here for; to make us stronger, better organized personalities; and to create in us an undying faith in the redemptive power of God in his world. Winning losers, successful failures, with God!

I BELIEVE IN MAN

I

WE FREQUENTLY HEAR it said in our day that man is done for, that his powers are unequal to his tasks, that the future of the human enterprise looms uncertain. This spirit of distrust is in open contrast to the confidence in man expressed in the Scriptures. A good example of this is our text, the words of Moses in his farewell address to the Israelites:

> "For this commandment which I command you this day is not too hard for you, neither is it far off. It is not in heaven, that you should say, 'Who will go up to heaven, and bring it to us, that we may hear it and do it?' Neither is it beyond the sea, that you should say, 'Who will go over the sea for us, and bring it to us, that we may hear it and do it?' But the word is very near you; it is in your mouth and in your heart, so that you can do it."
>
> DEUTERONOMY 30:11-14

Do you catch the spirit of that ancient utterance? After challenging his people to what must have seemed to them an idealistic task all but impossible of accomplishment, Moses said, "This undertaking is not beyond your powers. God is not asking some-

29

thing of you that you are incapable of performing. You are equal to the divine tasks assigned you. You can do it." Have we any reasons to share Moses' confidence in the human enterprise? I am convinced that we do.

II

1. I believe in man because of the central place he occupies in the natural world.

The favorite pastime of some people in our day is to belittle man, to downgrade him, to discount his importance. James Branch Cabell once said, "Man is a parasite infesting the epidermis of a midge among the planets." Whatever our judgment of the rest of his statement, we must agree that he is correct when he says man lives on the surface of a midge among the planets. In fact he is a mere mote on the midge. Van Loon opens his geography with the calculation that if everybody in the world were six feet tall, one and a half feet wide and one foot thick, then the whole human race (some two or more billion of us) could be packed into a box measuring half a mile in each direction. He then goes on to say that if we were all so packed and the box were taken to the Grand Canyon of Arizona and pushed over, it would tear and rip its way to the bottom with considerable noise and make a big splash as it hit the Colorado River at the bottom, but the noise would not be audible at any great distance. Certainly it would have little effect on the canyon itself. Astronomers on distant and nearby planets, if there be such, would have noticed nothing out of the ordinary. "And a century from now, a little mound, densely covered with vegetable matter, would perhaps indicate where humanity lay buried."

That's enough to humble our human pride, or, to change the figure of speech, to take some of the wind out of human sails— if we are thinking only in terms of size. The whole human race together is a mere speck compared to the earth on which it exists and the earth is a mere speck among the starry hosts of heaven. Why then should we consider ourselves of any importance in the vast scheme of things? For the simple reason that size is not the only, nor necessarily the most significant, method of measuring importance, much less of estimating quality. Size may be a handicap, as Alice discovered when she found herself too large to enter an enticingly beautiful garden in Wonderland. Scientists believe that the prehistoric animals of prodigious strength and mountainous size became extinct because of their bulk. They were superseded by smaller animals with agility, speed, and finely balanced instincts. A mother very properly reminded her child of his worth as compared to the material world of which he is a part when she said to him at bedtime,

"If the wonderful World is so great to you,
And great to father and mother, too,
You are more than the Earth though you are such a dot!
You can love and think, and the Earth cannot!"

WILLIAM BRIGHTLY RANDS

Long ago Pascal said, "Man is the feeblest reed in nature, but he is a reed that thinks. It is not necessary that the entire universe should arm itself to crush him. A vapour, a drop of water, suffices to kill him. But though the universe should crush him man would still be more noble than that which kills him because he knows that he dies, while the universe knows nothing of the advantage which it has over him." You can hardly measure the quality of man's mind, nor the power of his reason, his conscience, and his emotions with scales and a yardstick. He compasses the universe in thought. He commands and controls forces infinitely more powerful than his own strength. He defies space and time with the power of his imagination, and now even with the ingenuity of his space machines. He puts to shame all the rest of creation by the quality of his sacrifices. What, then, is the measure of man?

Immediately after the sinking of the "Titanic" someone drew a cartoon in two parts to interpret the event. In the first picture he showed the giant steamer, the finest boat afloat up to that

time, the most luxuriously furnished, the most expensive ever
built, ripped asunder by the collision with the iceberg. The pride
of human ingenuity crushed like a piece of paper by one stroke
of nature's little finger. All about are hundreds of human beings
floundering in the dark waters. Underneath is the caption, "The
supremacy of nature, the weakness of man!" In the second picture
a cross section of the deck of the sinking ship is shown. A strong
young man is yielding his seat in the lifeboat to a weak little
woman. As she takes the boat he steps back on the deck of the
sinking ship with a smile on his face. Underneath *this* picture is
the caption, "The weakness of nature, the supremacy of man!"

> Know, man hath all which Nature hath but more;
> And in that more lie all his hopes of good . . .
> Man must begin, know this, where nature ends.

The most significant experiment Nature is making is taking
place inside the personalities of men. There Nature is experi-
menting with something not found elsewhere in her vast scheme:
with reason, conscience, free willpower, controlled emotions,
the creative power of self-directing personalities and all the values
that accrue from the social relationships of such beings. Rufus
Jones once put it this way: "The whole universe is the basis and
framework for the spiritual adventure going on in man." Man
produces what no other creature on this earth can produce:
mind-stuff, soul-stuff, personality-stuff. That makes him an actor
in a drama vastly larger than his own little life. If these things
are of more importance than icebergs and blind instincts, then
size shrinks into insignificance, and quality becomes the biggest
thing of which the universe can boast.

Nature is functioning at her highest level in man. One writer
says, "Man is a physico-chemico—physiological-psychical-social
functioning of the original cosmic material." All modifications
and extensions of Nature made by the mind of man, all that
he adds to what Nature achieves without him, are part and parcel
of the natural order itself. These achievements are not unnatural,

but are the forms that Nature assumes as she operates through man. If the soil grows trees, man grows ships, motor cars, airplanes, space vehicles, paintings, musical instruments, books, hospitals, schools, churches, and political societies. When measured in terms of materiality man may be small, but, measured in terms of personality, there is nothing greater and more important in creation than he.

2. I believe in man because I subscribe to the biblical doctrine of man.

For all we know, Emerson might have had the words of Moses in mind when he wrote:

> So nigh is grandeur to the dust,
>   So near is God to man;
> When duty whispers low, "Thou must,"
>   The youth replies, "I can."

In the creation story in Genesis we have the first known theory of evolution. Some unknown writer says that God created the world in great stages, from the lowest to the highest, and that at the top stands man, who was created in God's own image (Gen. 1). The writer of the 8th Psalm stood amazed at man in comparison to the mystery and wonder of the heavenly bodies at night when the moon is full. Then he adds—a most significant sentence: "Yet [in comparison] Thou hast made him little less than God, and dost *crown* him with glory and honor" (v. 5). The language experts tell us that the expression, "Thou hast made him little less than God" (translated in the American Revised Version, "Thou hast made him little lower than God"), literally means, "Thou hast dropped him a little lower than God." This is an interesting picture: In the process of creation God was dropping things out of heaven—rocks a long way from himself, plants a little less far away, animals still less far away, but man was dropped but a very little lower than himself. Throughout the Old Testament we are told that God is involved in the affairs of the human race—that he loves, disciplines, guides, and otherwise shows his fatherly interest in their lives.

In the New Testament that doctrine is developed still further. There it is declared that when God started the universe on its long and costly journey He had in mind the ultimate emergence of men made in his image, redeemed by his grace, developed into Christlike personalities, through whom the whole world will become his kingdom. In short, our biblical faith is that man is the key to the whole creative process. The universe is not only favorable to this undertaking, constantly backing it up, but the universe initiated it and is actually engaged in it. There is a moral imperative, built into the very structure of man's being, not to fail his Maker, but to be a worthy partner of his Cosmic Companion in working towards that

> One far off divine event
> To which the whole creation moves.

Yes, we Christians dare to pitch our lives just that high. And we believe that in that grand conception is to be found the key to the mystery of the universe; in that doctrine is to be found the only philosophy big enough to encompass the whole process and explain it, comprehensive enough to justify its outlay of energy.

Hence we take sharp issue with all those modern pessimists who tell us that man is "a mere accident," "a little luminous meteor in an infinite abyss of nothingness," "a rocket fired on a dark night"; that "man is the product of causes which have no prevision of the end they are achieving"; that "his origin, his growth, his hopes and fears, his loves and his beliefs, are but the outcome of the accidental collocation of atoms"; that "there is no reason for man to suppose that his own life has any more meaning than the life of the humblest insect that crawls from one annihilation to another;" and that "ours is a lost cause and there is no place for us in the natural universe." Such are a few statements that I have been collecting from modern writers for some time past.

We Christians do not believe that man is an afterthought, a product of a blind universe operating by chance. We believe that he was planned for—that he has been cultivated, nourished, disciplined, loved by God from the beginning of time for His great and noble ends. Human life *does* have more meaning than that of the insects. We human beings, and we alone of all earthly creatures, can prevent the universe from being a mere collocation of atoms and cells. One young college student is reported to have prayed, "Lord, help me to be resigned to be an atom." Christians are taught and teach their youth to pray, "Lord, help me to become a free, self-directing, creative child of Thine."

3. I believe in man because I have faith in his ability to fulfilll his cosmic obligations.

There are plenty of ugly facts about men and sufficient cumulative evidence of their misdeeds, to make us wonder why they should have such a high conception of themselves. About the time we are sure they are going to be good, they suddenly decide to be filthy and foul. When you are certain they are trained to rule themselves by reason, they give rein to their emotions and become an unruly mob. When we suppose we are prepared to announce that they are thoroughly civilized, they revert to paganism. As their knowledge and wisdom accumulate we know they will profit by their past mistakes. Then, alas! they repeat over and over again the flagrant follies of their precedessors. "Man," said Eben Holden, "can be any kind of a beast, but a panther he can't be nuthin' but jest a panther." At one time or another man has outdone the beasts in expressing the many varieties of animalism of which the beasts are capable—so much so that Dostoevsky said that to speak of bestial cruelty is an insult to the beasts, for beasts can never be so "artistically cruel" as men.

But we must remember, as Emerson said, that "a man is like a bit of Labrador spar, which has no lustre, as you turn it in your hand, until you come to a particular angle; then it shows deep and beautiful colors." Turn this crude, unpolished, beastly thing

called man around. Behold another creature! Here are acts of
nobility, of courage, and of self-sacrifice that are the envy of the
angels! Here are products of his brain and brawn, his head and
heart, which make the gods claim him as their own. Man's pathway is strewn with his sordid sins and their consequences and with
his failings and follies. But his sins and failings are never final.
They shame him and stir him until he lifts his face toward the
stars. However deep he may descend into the pit, "nature grows
a vine in his soul that he may have something to take hold of to
climb out and have a clearer vision."

Mark Twain once cynically remarked, "Man is the only animal
that blushes—or needs to." That blush is an evidence of his greatness and a prophecy of his redemption. Walt Whitman said that
he envied the animals because

> They do not sweat and whine about their condition;
> They do not lie awake in the dark and weep for their sins;
> They do not make me sick discussing their duty to God;
> Not one is dissatisfied. . . .
> Not one is respectable or industrious over the whole earth.

That is why they are animals and why they remain so, and why
we should not envy them. That man is capable of being disturbed
by his own deeds is an indication of his superiority over all other
creatures. The very fact that he can sin also means that he has
potentialities for the free development of powers not possible
elsewhere in all organic life. Ants are a perfectly regimented
society. If that is what God wanted on the earth He could have
stopped there. He need not have gone to all the trouble, worry,
and outlay of energy to produce man. But He was aiming at
something finer. So He made us capable of resisting His will,
of rebelling against His wishes, of going astray from His way, of
refusing to choose His ideals.

Tennyson explained man's creation this way. God "let the
house of a brute to the soul of a man." But at the same time He
made it possible for man to "hold the sceptre, and rule the

province," sublimate the wishes of the body to the ideals of the soul, until at last "there is heard no yelp of the beast," and man can stand "on the heights of his life with a glimpse of a height that is higher."

At least that is our Christian faith. We believe that, with the help of God, it is possible to realize our noblest potentialities. To believe that, to hold tenaciously to that faith, is the ladder by which we rise "from the lowly earth to the vaulted skies," the tool by which we turn our potentialities into actualities. Call it egotism if you wish, but man believes that he is better than the beasts, more than material forces which play about him, capable of sublimer heights than he has hitherto attained. He feels himself called to share the purposes of the cosmos itself. He has an unquenchable thirst for oneness with God. With an ever-enlarging consciousness of his own worth he dares to declare himself like unto his Maker, to say that his spirit is a breath of the Divine, to believe himself destined to be a co-worker with God and to venture forth courageously on his divine tasks. Human beings persist with Peter in calling themselves "an elect race, a royal priesthood, a holy nation, a people for God's own possession" (I Peter 2:9). If that be swollen pride, make the most of it. But we insist that we are not made of ordinary stuff and therefore not made for ordinary living. Our pride is the lever by which we pry ourselves to better living. Again and again our human race has come back when it was regarded as done for. Out of the ashes of ruined civilizations has arisen a better social order. You cannot crush hope in man's breast, nor kill his morale, nor conquer his spirit, nor rob him of his dreams. His egotism is his means of emergence from his fallen estate and of his entrance into higher realms.

That faith in our human kind is essential to the success of the human enterprise. If we do not lose it there is no justification for the belief that human civilization is a lost cause. Nothing stands in the way of human progress except human beings. The greatest enemy of mankind is man. There is nothing outside us that compels us to throw away the achievements of our race. Moses was

right: we need not be asking how we can get a visitor from
heaven, from some other planet, or from some other part of the
world to come and show us how to perform our divine assign-
ment. The ability to do this is right here, in our own minds,
hearts and souls. That job is not too hard for us. We can do it!

III

It is the supreme function of our Christian faith to give us
inspiration and encouragement, and to equip us with the energy
for this undertaking. Before we are bidden to work for a goal it
was God's goal. Our dreams are not born of our wishful fancies.
They are part of us, born with us, part of our spiritual heritage.
And we dare to believe that God thinks so much of us and of the
experiment He is making through us that He shares its responsibility with us. He does not quit because we make mistakes,
commit blunders, and become rebellious. He loves us with a
neverfailing love. He empowers us for our work. He will see the
venture through with us to the end. "Go . . . and I am with you
always to the close of the age," our Lord promised.

Someone has said that the human enterprise is not an evolution, a rolling out of the past, but an ad-volution, a turning
toward something previsioned. We are not being blindly pushed
from behind, God is pulling us forward from before. He is out
ahead, leading, eternally struggling for us and with us until we
reach the goal He set for us from the beginning of creation. And
always we acknowledge as did Paul, "not that we are sufficient
of ourselves to claim anything as coming from us; our sufficiency
is from God" (II Cor. 3:5).

THANKSGIVING AND
THANKSLIVING

What shall I render to the Lord for all his bounty to me?
—PSALM 116:12

I

I HAVE CHOSEN Psalm 116 as the basis of this sermon, because a proper understanding of this psalm is calculated to arouse in us the mood we need to observe suitably our national Thanksgiving Day.

The value of the psalms for the Christian cannot be exaggerated. There is hardly any mood of the human soul that does not find its counterpart in some psalm. Luther called the Psalter "a Bible in miniature," because, said he, "All things which are set forth more at length in the rest of the scriptures are collected into a beautiful manual of wonderful and attractive brevity." Calvin said: "This book I am wont to call an anatomy of all parts of the soul; for no one will find in himself a single feeling of which the image is not reflected in this mirror. Here the Holy Spirit has represented to the life all the griefs, sorrows, fears, doubts, hopes, cares, anxieties, in short, all the stormy emotions, by which human minds are wont to be agitated."

Every Christian should be so familiar with the individual psalms that he can readily recall a psalm that fits his spiritual needs for any particular occasion. This is the reason why the

39

Book of Psalms is the most widely used collection of religious poems to be found in any land or language. Practically all of them are suitable for spiritually therapeutic purposes.

So to try to put us in the mood which should characterize the Thanksgiving season I wish to introduce you to Psalm 116, one of the outstanding thanksgiving psalms.

The person who wrote this psalm was, or thought he was, in imminent danger of dying. Whether he was gravely ill or in peril on the battlefield or threatened with personal violence we do not know. All the writer tells us is that he was so near death that he could feel himself slipping into Sheol. In those days Sheol was supposed to be the dark, gloomy abode of the dead. It was pictured as a foreboding and forbidding place where the spirits of men continued to exist in some shadowy manner but without any of the sensations which characterized their earthly life.

In his extremity the psalmist did what most of us would do under similar conditions: he prayed. He asked God to save him. And, his prayer was answered: he did not die. Ever afterward he declared that God stepped into the situation and snatched him from the jaws of death. No person can go through an experience like that without doing some serious thinking about the meaning and the mystery of life, without feeling how utterly futile our human efforts and ingenuity are at times, how utterly dependent we are on forces beyond our control, how necessary it is to believe in a power not ourselves that sustains and shapes our lives. The psalmist saw life anew, saw it "steadily and saw it whole," in its proper proportions, in its relationship to God. Having all but lost life, he began to prize it above his chief joy. He wanted nothing so much as just to live. He realized that hitherto life must be lived as a great obligation. He must somehow match his appreciation with acts that would justify God in giving him a new lease on life, a new opportunity to live it.

He sat down and put his decisions into a poem which all his contemporaries could read. It is one of the most intensely personal of all the psalms. He said to himself: "Return, O my soul, to your rest, for the Lord has dealt bountifully with you" (v. 7).

Then he asked himself, "What shall I [personally] render to the Lord for all his bounty to me?" (v. 17). It is as if he were saying to himself, "How can I ever be grateful enough to God? How can I ever express my appreciation to him?" Having asked his question, he proceeded to answer it. In the course of his poem he tells how he vowed to do three things: to *express* his thanksgiving, to *enjoy* life to the fullest, and to *dedicate* himself to God publicly, before the whole congregation of his people.

II

1. What shall I render to the Lord for all his bounty to me?" Thanksgiving:

"I will offer him the sacrifice of thanksgiving," that is, "I will publicly express my thanksgiving."

There is something lacking in the character of a person who never has any urge to thank someone for life and its varied experiences. There is no such thing as a self-made man. No person can claim literally, "I am the master of my fate, the captain of my soul." Paul asked the Corinthians, "What have you that you did not receive?" (I Cor. 4:17). The true answer to this must be, "Little or nothing." We arrive in this world completely equipped as body-personality beings who are the product of numerous forces with which we had nothing whatever to do. Life is sustained and often shaped by forces which are wholly outside our jurisdiction. We have little to do with the actual production of the necessities of our life. Not one of us lives entirely by his own efforts, not even the farmer. The social order in which we "live and move and have our being" is given. It is folly to boast that we keep ourselves alive. At any moment our lives could be terminated by something going wrong within the mechanism of our bodies, or by some external catastrophe which all of us pooling our resources would be helpless to prevent. Life itself, the whole order of nature, the society of people, the economic order, the cultural order, the educational order, the religious order, all the noblest values and ideals of the race—all these are given. Each of us inherits them. We are the products of the labors, the sacrifices, the struggles, the sufferings, of thousands of people who lived before us and who live all about us. What have we that we did not receive? *Nothing! !*

Have we no desire to express gratitude for all these things? In the 17th century during the epidemic known as the "black death," when London was all but decimated and life in the city was disrupted, Richard Baxter told in his journal how the people were so frightened that they avoided each other as they went down the streets. Then he added: "O how sinfully unthankful we are for our quiet society, habitation and health." Is there any sin worse than the sin of unthankfulness, ingratitude?

As I look back—and believe me there are values in having lived long enough to view life with the perspective of decades— the evidence of how little we have to do with our own "fates" becomes cumulative and impressive. Doors that I tried to open closed in my face. At the most unexpected moments, and wholly apart from my own efforts, doors opened before me as by an invisible hand, and I could all but hear a voice behind me saying, "This is the way. Walk in it." My life was diverted *from* certain things, channeled *into* certain courses, by some power or powers not my own. I can even see clearly where I could have gone astray, but did not, thanks to something other than myself. Again and again I have read and shared the mood of these lines written by William Dean Howells,

> Lord, for the erring thought
> Not unto evil wrought;
> Lord, for the wicked will
> Betrayed and baffled still;
> For the heart from itself kept;
> Our thanksgiving accept.

Convinced that I have many valid reasons for doing so, I attribute these things to God. And when I list the things for which I am grateful I end, as did Joyce Kilmer, by saying, "And, O thank God for God." During the London blitz, when the children were sent out into the rural districts to insure that there would be another generation of Britishers, a little girl in her foster home was heard to end her bedtime prayer with this plea, "And please, dear God, take good care of yourself, for if anything happens to you, we are sunk." Why not? That's good theology! In my judgment it is thoroughly biblical theology.

I say again, there is something deficient in the character of that person who can live in this marvelous, mysterious universe, with all its glorious opportunities and its varied and exciting experiences, and feel no urge to thank somebody for it. He needs what Robert Louis Stevenson called the experienced hand of a "Celestial Surgeon" to perform a spiritual operation on his soul.

> If I have faltered more or less
> In my great task of happiness;
> If I have moved among my race
> And shown no glorious morning face;
> If beams from happy human eyes
> Have moved me not; if morning skies,
> Books, and my food, and summer rain
> Knocked on my sullen heart in vain:—
> Lord, thy most pointed pleasure take
> And stab my spirit broad awake.
> (From "The Celestial Surgeon")

2. "What shall I render to the Lord for all his bounty to me?" Enjoyment:

"I will walk before the Lord in the land of the living" (v. 9).

That is practically equivalent to saying, "I will enjoy living." The scholars tell us that the psalmist's pledge literally means "I will walk before the Lord in the land of living people." Having been delivered from the shadowy land of Sheol, he now proposes to make the most of his opportunity to live in *this* world, this world of human beings. It is as though he were saying, "From

now on I'm really going to make the most of living, going to live
ordinary human life appreciatively and enthusiastically." Con-
sidering the setting, the contents, and the mood of his poem, I
think we can legitimately imply that he means to give the im-
pression, "For the rest of my days on this earth I mean to enjoy
life among my fellows, to live it with zest and to live it radiantly."

But note! This has no resemblance to the person who, realizing
that he has escaped death, decides to turn himself loose, to let
himself go, to live it up, to celebrate by giving a rowdy, hilarious
party with dissipated companions. No! ! The psalmist specifies
what kind of living he intends to display. He states emphatically
that he intends to "walk before the Lord," to live his life as God
intended it, to conform his ways to God's will, to make glad the
heart of his Maker. Remember: the psalmist is describing what
he proposes to do to express his gratitude to God, namely, to
prove his gratitude by the quality of his daily living.

Unfortunately, and quite mistakenly, some Christians seem to
think that it is somehow unbecoming, or perhaps even sinful, to
be too enthusiastic about ordinary human living, too happy about
life in these fleshy bodies in this material universe. One Greek
word translated "blessed" in our English New Testament is
makarious, which literally means "happy." The translators of
scripture have never been willing to use this in its literal meaning,
e.g., in the Beatitudes—"Happy are the poor in spirit . . . the
meek . . . the merciful," etc. Why? Apparently on the ground that
it is not quite respectful to our Master or to the other writers of
the sacred New Testament scriptures to speak of Christians as
"happy." That word is a little too earthy, or human, or anthropo-
morphic. In I Timothy 1:11 Paul speaks of "the glorious gospel
of the *makarious* God, with which I have been entrusted." And,
of course, the translators couldn't think of translating it the "glorious gospel of the happy God." Why, I ask you, are we unwilling
to attribute happiness to the God and Father of our Lord, Jesus
Christ, who came into the world as a little baby, and took upon
himself human flesh and was tempted in all points that we are?
We attribute other human emotions to God, notably love, for

example. Then why not happiness? I think it was Gilbert K. Chesterton who once said that he liked to think of God getting a thrill out of saying to the sun afresh every morning, "Come up again, come up again."

Be that as it may, of this I am sure, it is a false interpretation of the Christianity of the New Testament to say that Christians should depreciate life in their physical bodies, that we should regard it as a sin to enjoy living human life in all its aspects and with zest.

In his parables Jesus likened the kingdom of God to a person who found a pearl of great price, and to another person who found a valuable treasure hidden in the field, both of whom were willing to give all they had to procure these valuables and did so with "joy." Did not Jesus say, "I came that they [my followers] may have life and have it abundantly"? (John 10:10). The scholars tell us that when John uses the expression "eternal life," he means life of a certain quality that has its beginning here and now in this mundane world, not simply life after death. Paul said that God ". . . richly furnishes us with everything to enjoy" (I Tim. 6:17). He also said that our "bodies" are the temple of the Holy Spirit and that we ought to glorify God in our bodies (I Cor. 6:19). And never forget that he said this in connection with his discussion of sex. Somehow we modern Christians have either lost the radiance of our religion or have never experienced it as did the early Christians. Perhaps we have never dared to launch out on our faith, to exploit it, to put it to the test.

To enter zestfully into human life, to enjoy living in this world among our fellows, and to pour the best we have into living it as God intended it, is not a sin, but a great opportunity, a great challenge. One of the best ways we can thank God for life is to live it well and to enjoy doing it.

I challenge you to sit down sometime before Thanksgiving, and make three lists of the things that you really are—or ought to be —grateful for. (1) A list of all the amazing powers entrusted to us human beings: the joys that flow from our human society, the pleasures of our several senses, the moral and spiritual possibilities wrapped up in our personalities. When this list is made I think you will want to burst out with something comparable to what Browning once wrote:

> How good is man's life, the mere living, how fit to employ
> All the heart and soul and senses forever in joy!

(2) A list of the numerous blessings that are ours simply because we are privileged to live in the United States of America. When this list is finished I hope you will want to get down on your knees and say, "Thank you, God, for America," and then to arise and sing "My Country 'Tis of Thee," or "America the Beautiful." (3) A list of the special blessings which are ours as believers in Christ. Upon the completion of this list I trust you will want to burst out with something like these lines from the Scottish Psalter based on Psalm 103:

> Bless, O my soul, the Lord thy God
> And not forgetful be
> Of all the gracious benefits
> He hath bestowed on thee.

After that, I trust you will be in a mood that prompted Joseph Addison to write:

> Ten thousand, thousand, precious gifts
> My daily thanks employ;
> Nor is the least a cheerful heart
> That tastes those gifts with joy.

3. "What shall I render to the Lord for all his bounty to me?" Dedication:

"I will lift up the cup of salvation and call upon the name of the Lord" (v. 13); "I will pay my vows to the Lord in the presence of his people" (vv. 14, 18); "O Lord, I am thy servant" (v. 16).

The psalmist said more about dedication than about any other method of showing gratitude. God's very goodness purchased him to a life of loyalty to God. That is the highest form of thanksgiving. Thanksgiving is not merely saying something "nice" to God, or enjoying what he has so generously given us, but, as one person put it, "the *habitual* recognition of life as a great obligation."

More than any other group in the world we Christians ought to be aware of this. For, as Paul reminded us, "We are not our own; we are bought with a price," the price of God's suffering, forgiving, redeeming love in Christ. We are purchased to be what Paul calls a "living sacrifice": ". . . Yield yourselves to God," Paul said, "as men who have been brought from death to life, and your members to God as instruments of righteousness" (Rom. 6:13). This can also be called "dedicated living," a lifelong dedication of all that we are and have.

When he was only twenty years of age William E. Gladstone, the famous English statesman, expressed in his diary that determination "that the life of God may become the habit of my soul." That's it!! Someone said of Chiang Kai-Shek that he had "an incurable habit of using his religion literally as a secular way of life." That's it!! John Baillie once said, "My earliest memories have a definitely religious atmosphere. I cannot recall a time when I did not feel in some dim way that I was not my own to do with as I pleased, but was claimed by a higher power which had authority over me." Someone listed all the things for which he was grateful and then called them the things that bring "a pride in living and a boundless debt."

Thanksgiving is not properly expressed unless it leads to thanksgiving, unless each of us like the psalmist and like those Christians I have just mentioned, makes his vows in the presence of the people: that so long as he lives, he pledges himself to live as God's instrument, as one who is no longer his own but God's; that he expects daily to show his colors, raise his flag, let everybody know whose he is and whom he serves, that he is proud to bear the "brand of Christ." In his epistles Paul describes Christians as those upon whom God has put his "seal," or those who have been "sealed" for God's redemption by the Holy Spirit (II Cor. 1:22; Eph. 1:13; 4:30). The ultimate and final act of thanksgiving for what God has done for us in Christ and in the Holy Spirit is the surrender and the dedication of ourselves, saying,

> Here's my heart, O take and seal it,
> Seal it for thy courts above.

III

Take a final look at precisely what the psalmist asked and the answers he gave: "What shall *I* render to the Lord for all his bounty to *me?* "*I* will offer him the sacrifice of thanksgiving" . . . "*I* will walk before the Lord in the land of the living"; "*I* will pay my vows to the Lord now in the presence of his people"; "O Lord, *I* am thy servant." Thanksgiving is a personal matter, an individual matter. Each of us has a life that only he can live, an obligation that only he can fulfill, a debt that only he can pay.

> Love so amazing, so divine,
> Demands *my* soul, *my* life, *my* all.

THE WAY

Saul, still breathing threats and murder against the disciples of the Lord, went to the high priest and asked him for letters to the synagogue at Damascus, so that if he found any belonging to the Way, men or women, he might bring them bound to Jerusalem.

—ACTS 9:1-2

I

THIS IS ONE of six places in the Book of Acts where the followers of Jesus were spoken of as belonging to "the Way." (Cf. Acts 19:9; 19:23; 22:4; 24:14; 24:22.) In these passages the word "way" is capitalized in both the American Revised and the Revised Standard Versions of the Bible to distinguish its use as a title for the early Christian movement from its use in the ordinary sense. Before the followers of Jesus were called "Christians" (Acts 11:26) they were called members of "the Way."

When outsiders applied the term to Christians they might well have been referring to a variety of things: their way of thinking about God; their worship practices; their way of organizing for religious activities; the manner in which they conducted themselves in their homes, in the market places, in social groups; their attitudes toward marriage, toward the opposite sex, toward social customs, toward other faiths and races, toward the Roman government—in short, their mode of living, their total way of life.

It should never be forgotten that genuine Christianity is, or should be, *a way of life*—a specific, particular, distinctive type or

49

quality of life. Let us take a good, hard look at this central, but all-too-often-overlooked fact about our Christianity.

II

1. Christianity originated as a new way of life.

Professor Frederick C. Grant, a well-known biblical scholar, once described religion as "life controlled by the consciousness of God." Professor Ernest F. Scott, another noted scholar, speaking specifically of Christianity, called it "ethical theism." Both of these scholars were thinking of the same thing, namely, that one's belief in God provides a set of moral principles or values by which he ought to live in all his relations with his fellowmen, and both the desire and the ability actually to live by them.

The best way to discover how clearly Christianity came to the world as a way of life is to read at one sitting a series of selected New Testament passages without stopping to ask all the questions that arise, but only for the purpose of getting general impressions concerning precisely what it was the writers were trying to say concerning that new movement. Passages suitable for that purpose are as follows:

(1) *The Sermon on the Mount* (Matt. 5-7; Luke 6). This sermon is a lengthy explanation or exposition of the "righteousness" (which means "rightness" or "right living") which is acceptable to God and which should characterize those who subscribe to and profess to live by the gospel as proclaimed by Jesus. Sometimes it is said that the theme of this sermon is "The Ideal Life." It enjoins upon the hearers the duty of committing themselves to that way of life.

(2) *Six outstanding parables of Jesus* (Matt. 20:1-16, 25:14-46; Luke 10:25-37, 12:13-21, 16:19-31). Together with the other parables of Jesus these constitute another large block of material in the Gospels which illustrates the motivations, qualities, values and purposes that are characteristic of those who call themselves Christians.

(3) *The Christian doctrine of creation* (Rom. 6:1-14 and 8:18-23). In these passages Paul reminds his fellow Christians that God's purpose in creating and redeeming the human race was to develop them into the sons of God, who will "walk in newness of life."

(4) *The Christian doctrine of vocation* (Rom. 12). Here Paul urges Christians to remember that it is their special calling in the world to live "dedicated" lives, to put "spiritual" qualities (which are listed in vv. 9-21) to work in every area of the common life. It has well been said that Christianity is not a way of doing certain things but a certain way of doing everything.

(5) *The Christian doctrine of love* (I Cor. 13). The doctrine is stated and then a list is given of the desirable qualities a love-dominated person exhibits and the undesirable qualities he rejects.

(6) *Distinguishing characteristics of Christians:* (a) Christian graces that the "new men in Christ" are supposed to "put on" (Gal. 5:16-24); (b) practices that Christians are supposed to "put off" (Col. 3:5-10); (c) cumulative fruits supposed to be produced in a growing Christian's life (II Pet. 1:3-8).

No one who reads these suggested passages in quick succession can fail to understand why the early Christian movement was labeled "the Way," a *distinctive* way of living.

Church historians tell us that Christianity was able to win its way among the numerous religions then in existence in the Roman Empire precisely because of the quality of the lives of its adherents: their monogamous marriages, their superior family life, their responsible social living, their high moral standards, their brotherliness.

One of the oldest Christian documents, outside the New Testament, now extant (c. A.D. 100) is a letter written by an unknown person to another person addressed as Diognetus, in which, among other things, he said: "What the soul is to the body, that Christians are to the world. The soul is dispersed through all the members of the body, and Christians are scattered through all the cities of the world." The implication is that Christians were pouring new life into the society in which they lived and labored.

A modern way of saying the same thing would be that Christians are the bloodstream of society, that just as the blood circulates throughout the body, giving life to every part of the body, so Christians do in their world.

2. The Christianity of too many church members in modern times seems to be divorced from their practical lives.

One of the most disturbing, disheartening things to Christian leaders in the West is that so many professing Christians appear not to connect their religion with their morals and ethics. An alarmingly large number of active church members are among those who are being convicted in our courts of embezzling money, taking and offering bribes, cheating on income tax returns, and a variety of other unscrupulous dealings. A senior at Radcliffe College is reported recently to have said, "I believe in God but it doesn't affect my life." The question is: does she, can she really believe in God unless that belief affects the quality of her life?

If there is one aspect of the current moral trends that is more disturbing than another, it is that so many Christians seem not to have any feeling of obligation to serve God in and through their vocations. The wife of a minister, talking to a reporter about her husband's career, said, among other things, "He relinquished his profession as a design engineer to enter the service of God." On the surface this implies that a person cannot serve God as a design engineer, but must engage in specifically religious work to do this. A Christian businessman told a person making a survey that he had two codes of ethics, one for the world in which he engages in business, the other for his "spiritual" work in the church. I once heard the editor of a large metropolitan newspaper say to a group of Boy Scout executives, "I make my living as editor of the paper. I serve God by working in the Scout movement." As if he couldn't do both—and shouldn't be expected to do both—at the same time.

Protestant churches have never had so many members, so

much expensive equipment and such large budgets. In recent years they have been experiencing a revival of religion of a sort. The tragedy is that just at a time when they are strongest in many other respects they are weakest in performing the basic work of producing Christians who make it their divine vocation to put their Christianity to work in their daily lives.

3. What the Church can do to encourage Christians to put their religion to work in their common life.

How can we account for this widespread discrepancy between the formal professions of Christians and the quality of their deeds? What can the Church do to change the situation? Actually this is not a new development in religion. Human nature being what it is, we cannot expect one hundred percent consistency between people's professions and their deeds in any age. Jesus labeled many of the religious leaders of his day "hypocrites." He once asked his enthusiastic followers wistfully, "Why do you call me Lord, Lord, and not do what I tell you?" (Luke 6:46).

There is no single explanation for the present predicament of the Christian churches in our country and no simple cure for it. It has undoubtedly been developing over a fairly long period of time, and is the result of a combination of factors. But we can make a few observations that are relevant and worthy of consideration.

(1) *It can simply reorganize its ecclesiastical "machinery."*

Protestant churches in recent years have been increasingly becoming over-organized. The number and kinds of subsidiary organizations and activities in these churches have been mounting so rapidly that the mere operation of the machinery of churches demands a disproportionate amount of the time, energy and resources of their members, ministers and officials. Some of these activities are quite in harmony with the main purposes of Christian churches, but some should be regarded as more or less peripheral. Others duplicate or compete with secular organizations that serve the special needs—cultural, educational, recreational, political, physical, economic and sociological—of various age and interest groups in the community.

The time is ripe for someone whose word carries weight in Protestantism to say to Protestant churches, "Discocoon yourself," an expression coined by Dr. Halford E. Luccock of Yale Divinity School. Churches sorely need to disentangle themselves from their complicated extracurricular activities so they can devote their major time, energies, and resources to their main educational job.

(2) *It can reformulate its conceptions of its distinctive role in society.*

The big question is, of course, precisely what is the Church's main job? To answer that question Protestant denominations of our time need to restudy and restate their doctrine of the church, and to decide what is the distinctive work to which Christian churches have been divinely called and how that can best be fulfilled in the world.

The Church is not the Kingdom of God. It is not an end in itself, but a means to an end. It is not, or should not be, in competition with any other institution of society. It should not undertake to do the work of any other institution. It is not the Great Society itself. Its primary task is not to create the Great Society but to create the creators of that society. Its divine role is to keep its members aware of the claims of God on their lives, of their obligations to order all their personal and group life according to God's will as revealed in Christ, to motivate the members to do that will, and to help them find the spiritual resources to do it. That is why Jesus told his followers that they are the light of the world, the salt of the earth, the leaven in the dough. And we should never allow ourselves as churchmen to forget, as one pastor recently reminded his congregation, "that the church is supposed to be the leaven, not the lump." (Cf. Matt. 13:33.)

(3) *It can clarify for laymen where they can best serve the Church.*

Perhaps the most significant religious movement of the twentieth century is the Laymen's Movement. One of the purposes of this movement is to enlist laymen in the affairs and welfare of the Church. This is a noble and necessary project. But it has its dangers. Laymen so easily get the mistaken idea that their full Christian duties have been performed when they have assisted in raising the budget of the church, manned its various boards and agencies, promoted and participated in its subsidiary organizations and their activities, assisted the pastor in his pastoral functions, attended public worship, and occasionally assisted the minister by preaching and leading in worship.

In actuality, the most important contribution laymen can make to the work of their church takes place, not within the walls of the church buildings, but out in society where they engage in their life's work. Laymen should think of themselves as *the extended church*. The church really exists and is at work wherever a church member performs his particular daily tasks in the social order. Each person's daily work should become his Christian vocation in the sense that it is the major area of the world where he actually puts his Christian beliefs into practice. Laymen and they only are in a position to do this strategic work for the Kingdom of God. That is exactly where and how Christ's disciples become the salt of the earth, the light of the world, and the leaven that permeates the whole social order. The Kingdom of God can come in the earth only through those who live like Christians in every nook and corner of the workaday world. It can never be built by trying to make each local church the Kingdom of God in miniature.

(4) *It can give proper attention to commitment and spiritual disciplines in the life of the Church.*

Generally speaking, the major emphasis in most large Protestant denominations is now placed on recruiting new members and instructing them on what it means to be church members, rather than on persuading people to make personal confessions of faith in Christ and instructing them in what it means to be full-time Christians. Joining a church can—and often does— mean no more than joining a social club. It ought to involve not only a formal confession of one's faith but a personal commitment of one's life to Christ as Master and Lord. It is not, so to speak, a trial marriage but a union for life. This choice should involve the whole person—mind, will, emotions, all. This type of public profession of one's choice and commitment has become all but outmoded in many churches, because it is regarded as one of the methods of the old evangelism that should be discarded.

Furthermore, many churches no longer encourage their members to engage in prayer, Bible study, and the reading of devotional literature for spiritual therapeutic purposes, nor provide facilities for them to learn how to do so. On the contrary, these practices are discouraged as a form of false piety.

Is it surprising, then, that Christianity as a way of life has been lost sight of by so many church members when two ingredients— commitment and spiritual disciplines—are so commonly missing from their basic Christian training? Christian commitment of themselves to Christ—wholly meaningfully, emotionally, with all their hearts and minds and wills, for life, and unashamedly —provides the incentive and motivation for Christian living. Regular spiritual disciplines provide the inner resources essential for fulfilling the commitment.

III

There are two passages in the New Testament that contain illuminating figures of speech which contain the very essence of what I have been trying to say.

The first one is Philippians 3:20: "We are a colony of heaven" (Moffatt's translation). This statement has interesting implications. The historians tell us that Philippi was the center of a large Roman colony sent there to romanize the whole province of Macedonia with their own distinctive Roman customs and beliefs. Paul evidently knew this. So the Christians who received his letter to the Philippians knew the significance of his use of the word *colony*. In effect he was saying, "We [and note he included himself] Christians constitute another kind of colony. We are a colony of heaven. Our Master is not Caesar but Christ. Our job is to *Christianize* the world."

The second passage is I Peter 2:4-5: "Come to him, to that living stone, and like living stones be yourselves built into a spiritual house." Ordinary stones are dead. When laid in any place by the builder they remain inert. Try to imagine what a *living* stone would be like! Presumably when placed in position it would begin magically to produce other stones or enlarge itself and grow a foundation and a wall and finally a completed house. Wherever we Christians live we are supposed to be, each in his own sphere, each at his own special calling, the growing edge of a new society, the Kingdom of God.

OUR SPIRITUAL RESERVES

"And the foolish said to the wise, 'Give us some of your oil, for our lamps are going out.' But the wise replied, 'Perhaps there will not be enough for us and for you; go rather to the dealers and buy for yourselves.'"

—MATTHEW 25:8-9

I

I INVITE YOU to consider with me one of the best known, but I fear not always one of the best understood, of Jesus' parables: the parable of the ten maidens.

This parable has its setting in the wedding customs of the day. Weddings then customarily took place in the evening. The actual ceremony was usually at the home of the bride. After the ceremony, it was customary for the couple to proceed to their new home, walking along in all their finery under a bridal canopy. All the guests who desired to do so accompanied them. They took the longest way possible so that the people of the village might wish them well and, if they desired, present them with gifts. Along the way their friends, especially the young people, waited to join the procession. Those in the procession carried lamps consisting of a shallow bowl filled with oil, with a lip for the wick, mounted on some sort of upright holder. The procession resembled an old-fashioned torchlight parade. The festivities concluded with a feast in the couple's new home.

Upon this occasion, at a particular spot along the way, ten young maidens with their lamps were waiting to join the slowly-

moving procession. While waiting they fell asleep, since the festivities had been unduly prolonged. They were awakened by
someone saying, "They're coming!" Whereupon the maidens
arose, trimmed their wicks and made ready to join the marchers.
It chanced that five of them had forgotten to bring an extra
supply of oil for their shallow lamps. When they discovered their
lights were flickering and sputtering and going out, they turned
to the other five, who had wisely exercised foresight and brought
an extra supply of oil, and said, "Give us some of your oil." Their
answer was an emphatic "No! There might not be enough for
all of us. Go to the dealers where we got ours and buy for
yourselves." The five who had extra oil joined the procession.
While the five who had foolishly forgotten their extra oil had
gone to get it, the festivities began. Then when the five latecomers
reached the home, they found the door shut and bolted. The
doorkeeper refused to admit them.

Jesus seems to have used this simple story to stress the need of
a reserve supply of moral and spiritual resources. The refusal
of the five to share their extra supply of fuel with the other five,
and of the host to open the door to the late arrivals, sounds severe.
I have no doubt that Jesus meant it to sound so. There is a severe
aspect to the Gospel that our generation has almost forgotten.
The necessity of having inner resources, our inability to borrow
them from others, and the personal and social tragedies that result
from not possessing them in an emergency—all these are solemn
truths, worth our careful consideration.

II

*1. This parable emphasizes the importance of possessing inner
resources.*

Life is not easy. Any person makes a grave mistake who sup-
poses that life is a Fourth of July picnic, or a weekend party, or

who, in the language of an old hymn, expects "to go to heaven on flowery beds of ease." Life can be grand and glorious, romantic and thrilling—and should be—but it is never easy.

It is hard to make a living and keep on making it until the end. It is hard to keep in health, to build a home, to form a character, and to make a success of your life's work. Those who have been fighting the battle of life for some decades know what I mean. Life makes a continuous demand upon the best resources we can command. It subjects our inner man to constant strains and stresses, as a house is subjected to the ravages of the elements and time. One must prod himself; keep his human relations in good repair; struggle daily with his conscience and against discouragement, inertia, and self-satisfaction; develop his physical and moral energies; discipline his emotions; control his thoughts; generate faith, courage, morale and optimism; be vigilant against getting entangled in the trivialities and the details of the daily rounds. There is no place where he can stop and say to himself, "I have arrived; I've got it made; I'm fixed for life; I can take it easy." He cannot quit because he is tired and the going hard. To let up is to deteriorate, to vegetate, to wither at the roots, to throw away the talents with which he is endowed, to fail God, his fellowmen, and himself.

Some stand the strains of life and some do not. Life's pathway is literally strewn with the wrecks of human lives. The vicissitudes and changes, the sorrows and joys, tasks and tests, risks and duties, fortunes and misfortunes, successes and failures—the routine of living—are too much for some people. And down they go. Some go down in youth, some in adulthood, some in middle life, some in old age. It is sad but true that many people falter, fail, and fall.

But, thanks be to God, some people—numerous people, the great majority of them in fact—stand the strain of living and manage life quite successfully. In youth, in mature adulthood, through mid-life and down to old age, they fight the good fight nobly.

What is the difference between the two groups? We can state with assurance that the difference is not in the strains to which they are subjected, although it is characteristically human to think so. Generally speaking, all of us have the same tests and temptations from the outside. The difference is not in what takes place on the outside of us but what takes place on the inside. Face two people with identical obstacles: one will let the obstacle stop or divert him or turn him back; the other will find some way to overcome it. He will push it out of the way, detour around it, climb over it, drill through it. He will find some way to keep going ahead. The difference between the two people is what is in their inmost souls.

One of the characters in fiction says: "There ain't nothin' that walks that can lick us O'Haras—not hard times nor high taxes nor even downright starvation. . . . But we can be licked from the inside. What the world can't do, our own hearts can do. . . . That weakness that's in our hearts can lick us in the time it takes to bat your eye. . . . Everybody's mainspring is different. . . . Folks whose mainsprings are busted are better dead." Very well, what about the mainspring of your life, my friend?

What makes the failure of individuals so tragic is that, when they break down, the social machinery which is controlled by them breaks down, grinds to a halt, and fails. The Great Chinese Wall, erected to keep out hordes of enemies from the north, was breached three times in the first one hundred years, not from the outside but by betrayal from within. If our United States of America ever falls it will not be because of the assault by an outside enemy, but because of the deterioration of the moral fibre of its own citizens.

I don't like to deal in superlatives. But just now I say without hesitation that the most important need of our age is what I am talking about: an increase in the quantity and quality of the inner resources of our people—the resources within the soul that on the one hand restrain and on the other hand constrain; that undergird us, feed us with ideals, hopes, convictions, determinations and dreams; that drive out fears and anxieties and frustrations and pessimism and fatalism and despair. Just now America is already in the middle of a period when we and our institutions are being put to the severest tests of our history. Whether or not we stand the tests will depend upon what we have inside us—our spiritual resources.

It is said that a group of citizens sent a delegation to Washington to confer with their congressman about his stand upon some of the national issues before that body. After considerable discussion in which he had been taken to task for some of his positions, he said to them, "Gentlemen, you do not understand the outside pressures that are brought to bear upon us congressmen." Whereupon an old salt-of-the-earth Christian who was a member of the delegation blurted out, "Outside pressures? What about your inside braces?" What about *our* inside braces?

2. Next, the parable emphasizes the impossibility of borrowing inner resources from others.

There are some things we cannot borrow or buy from others and that others cannot give us or lend us or sell us. We wish this were not so. If only we could say to our children, as they move out into the world, "Here, take a little of my courage, my judgment, my patience, my moral willpower! You will need it while you are in college, in your marriage, in the practice of your life's work." We would like to do that just as we say to them at times, "Here, take this ten-dollar bill! You will need it on your trip." But that cannot be done. It is simply not possible for one person to give or sell or in any manner hand over his moral and spiritual resources to another. We can borrow our neighbor's tools, but not his strength and skill to use them. A successful businessman can pass on his capital, but not his capacity; his land, but not his ability to love; his farm, but not his faith; his money, but not his morals; his goods, but not his goodness; his cattle, but not his conscience.

Bishop Brent of the Episcopal church, who was a chaplain in the First World War, once said that the best sermon he ever heard was preached by a colonel of a regiment in the trenches in France. The Bishop had said what he thought was the most appropriate thing he could say to a group of men about to leave their trenches before daylight one morning to attack the enemy's positions, many of whom he knew would never come back. When he had finished the colonel arose and said, "Check your supply of shoelaces. When you are in the thick of battle you cannot depend upon your buddy's supply of shoelaces." Then he paused a moment and added, "Apply this to your spiritual needs." That was all, but it was enough. In the battle of life every man must depend upon his own supply of inner resources.

In John Bunyan's immortal allegory *Pilgrim's Progress,* the guide and the pilgrim come upon a scene where an old warrior is turning over the fight to a young soldier. He says, "My sword I give to him that succeeds me in my pilgrimage. My courage and skill to him that can get it." Exactly so! "Go to them that sell and buy for yourselves. Go, get it for yourself and pay the price." In this matter every person stands alone in the presence of God. The solemn truth is that there are no proxies for the soul.

3. Finally, the parable emphasizes the necessity for every person to get his own resources for himself from the source of supply.

All of us know people—perhaps because we are among them —who are careless, neglectful, dilatory, drifting along, procrastinating, counting on the resources of others, or their good luck, or something else, to get by. But in a crisis they find their supply of inner resources exhausted, their spiritual larder empty.

It is too late to have physical vitality if we wait until the dread disease strikes to try to get it. It is too late to have knowledge and skill to grasp the opportunity ahead if we have not gathered and stored them and assimilated them into life beforehand. It is too late to put stamina into our souls, courage into our wills, convictions into our consciences, and moral backbone into our characters if we wait until the temptation requiring those qualities faces us. Someone has said, "No man has any more religion than he can command in an emergency." That is undoubtedly true.

But it is also true that a man will have in an emergency only as much religion as he has put into his soul previously.

When in the parable Jesus said, or made the five maidens say, "Go and buy for yourselves," he implied, "There is only one way for each of us to secure spiritual reserves." How? By our regular, consistent, religious disciplines and habits. Spiritual resources are no more inherited or absorbed secondhand automatically from others around us than is knowledge. Just as we have to work to accumulate knowledge and to develop skills, so we have to work at the job of building up within us those resources we need: etching moral and social ideals on our minds, breeding convictions and beliefs, generating wholesome attitudes and emotions in our hearts, strengthening and reinforcing our wills. These things together constitute a method of developing a strong soul, just as physical exercise builds a strong body. This might aptly be called a hygiene for the soul.

Public worship, entered into thoughtfully, is one way of accomplishing these things. Never underestimate or minimize the importance of what you are doing by regularly attending public worship. But these same things are also accomplished in privacy when, through prayer and meditation, with the help of biblical passages, we keep "alive to God," Paul's way of expressing it; or "practice the presence of God," as the old mystics used to describe it; or establish "a confrontation between ourselves and God," as our generation of younger ministers like to speak of it. Each of us must do this for himself. Or, as the parable of Jesus put it, each of us has to get it where others have gotten it and pay the price.

The tragedy of our times is that these things are consistently neglected by too many of us who call ourselves Christians. To revert to the parable again, our "lamps," our inner lamps, are going out—flickering, sputtering, and dying out. All of us know the results of this. A slow moral and spiritual deterioration is going on in our land. It cuts across all classes and groups without exception. Each reader may fill in the details of this ugly picture for himself. And if you don't like the picture you see, I hope you will not say there is nothing you can do about it. For there is something each of us can do about it right now! We can say, "This moral and spiritual deterioration shall stop with me. I shall begin today to replenish my inner life where all the generations preceding ours have replenished theirs: from God, the eternal fountain of our moral and spiritual life." An old mystic used to say, "God must put his face against the windowpane of *our* lives." God *can* become that real to us.

> Speak to Him, thou, for He hears,
> And Spirit with spirit can meet,
> Closer is He than breathing,
> And nearer than hands and feet.

We are told that the difference between a magnet and an ordinary piece of steel is not in their strength. One has only its own strength but the other has the strength of the universe. In the ordinary steel the electrons have their positive and negative poles jumbled in such a way that they counteract and neutralize one another. In a magnet they are ordered so that all the positive poles point one way and all the negative the other way, and the whole current of the earth's magnetism can pass through. That is a parable of our inner lives. The moral and spiritual power of the universe is just as real as is magnetism, and it seeks to find a channel through our hearts. If we are willing for that to take place it will.

I do not hesitate to testify publicly today that I have felt God's power in my life. All too seldom, I grant you. But when I have so arranged my confused, jumbled inner life as to permit God's power to get through, that has been the only source of my inner strength. In those moments I have known what Paul meant when he said to the churches of Galatia, ". . . It is no longer I who live, but Christ who lives in me; and the life I now live in the flesh I live by faith in the Son of God . . ." (Gal. 2:20). Because of those moments I can subscribe to what Tennyson wrote:

> If e'er when faith had fallen asleep,
> I heard a voice, "believe no more"
> And heard an ever-breaking shore
> That tumbled in the Godless deep,
>
> A warmth within the breast would melt
> The freezing reason's colder part,
> And like a man in wrath the heart
> Stood up and answer'd, "I have felt."

Did not Jesus promise the woman at the well of Sychar that she could have the water of life, a supply that would become *in her* a spring of water—inexhaustible, never-failing, forever flowing—"welling up to eternal life" (John 4:13)? Yes, He did, and that is His promise still to us.

III

In Bunyan's allegory the pilgrim came to a place where a man was pouring water on a fire and could not put it out. His guide said to him, "Do you want to see the meaning of this strange sight? Come with me." He took the pilgrim around behind the fire and there on the back side another man was pouring oil on it. As fast as the man in front poured on water, the man behind poured on oil. The guide explained, "The oil represents the grace of God. When that keeps pouring into a man's soul its fires can never be quenched." When the grace of God gets a chance— keeps on getting a chance to come into our hearts—nothing can weaken or smother our inner life no matter what the outward circumstances may be. Because, as someone once said, "In every situation God and one man always—always—make a majority."

OUR CHANCE AT GREATNESS

Thus all the days of Methuselah were nine hundred and sixty-nine years; and he died.

—GENESIS 5:27

I

WHILE I WAS a professor in the seminary it was one of my responsibilities to try to help the students learn how to preach. During that time I read numerous books of sermons, old and new. I soon came to expect to find at least once a year a sermon on the text which I have chosen for this sermon. Invariably, the preacher, after announcing his text, would go on to say something like this: "Methuselah lived and died, that was all. In the long interval from his birth to his death he did nothing worth recording. His life had a single dimension—length. He merely existed. He didn't really live."

I submit that this is not a fair judgment of the man. To begin with, the historian uses precisely the same formula to conclude the statement about him as about the other men in his chronicle: that the total number of years he lived were so many and he died. In the next place, there are a number of facts given about him—briefly to be sure—but significant nevertheless. We are also told about what went before him and what came after him. When all these facts are taken into proper consideration we might well conclude that he was one of those souls who lived a good life without fanfare, performed his duties faithfully, carried on a great tradition, and who deserves to be called a really great man. At any rate, it is by living that sort of life that most of us get the only opportunity we will have to be great. That is the truth I invite you to consider with me now.

II

1. Methuselah appears to have qualified for honorable mention in the history books for his work behind the scenes.

The historian states that he married and had children and grandchildren. These are important facts. Rearing and supporting a family are not insignificant achievements. Under certain conditions they may be outstanding. If done properly, they require deeds of valor, and they bring forth in a person many of the elements of greatness. Millions of fathers and mothers have lived greatly but silently without being mentioned in the newspapers or in the books of history.

> I tell you the kingliest victories fought
> Are fought in these silent ways.

Indeed they are. And not only by mothers and fathers but by wives and husbands, sons and daughters, brothers and sisters, teachers and other professional people, and hosts of individuals in all walks and ways of life. Behind-the-scenes deeds of heroism and courage, lives of honesty and unselfishness, performed and lived by people who never received publicity nor sought it—that's what I'm talking about. Furthermore, they do not expect any credit or recognition. They just do their duty, live nobly, because they have consciences and feel divine obligations, and down in their hearts, know it is better to be good than evil, unselfish than selfish, honest than dishonest, and because they want to be happy and make others happy, to serve God and do their bit for His world.

On Ida M. Tarbell's eightieth birthday someone asked her to

name the greatest persons she had ever met. In her lifetime she had met many so-called great men and written the biographies of some of them. But to this request she responded, "The greatest persons I have ever met are those nobody knows anything about." Once the *New York Times* was asked to help a group of clubwomen decide on the twelve greatest women in the United States. After due consideration the editors replied, "The twelve greatest women in the United States are women who have never been heard of outside of their own homes."

Miss Tarbell and the editors of the *New York Times* were thinking of exactly the same thing: that one can live a great life and never be heard of outside the circle of his relatives and friends. Someone has said, "All of life can be lived out in a very little place." It can, indeed, and it is, for most of us. But that does not mean that our lives have either been wasted or are failures, and that we have not done important things. Not many of us will be remembered long after we are dead. Certainly we will not have our names written on the pages of history. It will not even be recorded there of us, as it was of Methuselah, that we lived and died. But that will not indicate that we have not had a full and useful, probably a great life.

Albert Edward Wiggam, the scientist, once said: "Thirty billion persons have been born since the dawn of recorded history. Of these only 5,000 ever amounted to much, and of the 5,000 supermortals less than 200 have been women." If one must qualify as a supermortal to amount to much the great masses of us are indeed doomed to failure.

But I ask you: who was greater, Thomas A. Edison or his mother? When he was a young lad his teacher sent him home with a note to his mother saying, "Your child is dumb. We can't do anything for him." She wrote back, "You do not understand my boy. I will teach him myself." And she did, with the results that are well known.

Who was greater, Henry Ward Beecher, the world-renowned preacher of the last century, or his school teacher? His sermons are among those still read and analyzed by students in our theological seminaries. When he had become internationally famous he stood in his pulpit in Brooklyn and publicly attributed his achievements to a woman who taught school for one term in the rural school he attended as a boy, and who, through understanding and skill, started him in the right direction. "But," he said to his congregation, "I have forgotten her name."

James Whitcomb Riley has a poem in which he tells of the death of a worker in a shop. He pictures his fellow workmen standing around on the day of his funeral talking about him. One man, after saying some complimentary things, with tears in his eyes while he said them, added, "When God made Jim, I bet He didn't do anything else that day but jest set around and feel good." I tell you, my friends, the only opportunity most of us will have to be great is to live so faithfully right where we are that God will "feel good" about having made us.

There are no lesser and greater in the eyes of God: only faithful and unfaithful servants. Christ said, "Blessed is that servant whom his Lord when he comes" will find watching, faithful, ready. Behind-the-scenes greatness! That's my first point.

2. Again, Methuselah seems to have won a place in history partly for the work he did indirectly.

Nothing is said of Methuselah except that he lived, married, had children, and died. But who were his children? We do not know much about any of them but Lamech, and we don't know anything about Lamech except that he was the father of Noah. So Methuselah was the grandfather of Noah. But we know a great deal about Noah. He was quite a man in his day. God chose him as the one through whom to preserve the human race. Conceivably we would not be here if it had not been for him. Noah had a great deal to put up with while he was building the ark. He was ridiculed and otherwise bemeaned. I have no doubt that in the midst of this his grandfather advised, counseled, encouraged, and supported him, and that Methuselah may be credited with having helped to make Noah a man whom God delighted to favor and honor—and that is exactly what the Bible says of Noah. Once someone wrote,

> The kind of a man I mean to be
> Is the kind of a man Mark Hopkins is.

I fancy, and I think it is not pure fancy, that again and again Noah said, "The kind of a man I mean to be is the kind of a man my grandfather Methuselah is."

Tennyson said of one of the Knights of the Round Table, "He laid his mind on theirs and they believed in his beliefs." Many a person has sat down with his children, or his grandchildren, or his friends, or his pupils or students, and laid his mind on theirs and caused them to believe in his beliefs. And down the line somewhere emerged great souls, great deeds which were the outcome of their efforts. And that is the way many of us can become great: by influencing someone else to become great.

A man in England dedicated a book to a friend with the words: "To J. Y. Simpson, who makes the best seem easily credible." Just as some men make the difficult seem possible, others make the best, the good, the honest, the honorable, the decent seem possible.

Someone has said that humanity will be saved by goodness propagating itself. Well, has anyone watched you and me and decided that goodness in all its best forms is possible in this sinful world? An old Presbyterian minister who was like a father to me in my early ministry, and who died many years ago in California, once preached a sermon with an outline which immediately caught the attention of the hearers and which they did not soon forget. Here it is: First point, "Have you got religion?" Second point, "Is it the catching kind?" Third point, "Has anybody caught it from you yet?" Has anybody "caught" true religion or anything else fine and good from you because of your influence upon him?—something that strengthens, enriches, undergirds him? Or, has he caught something that weakens, impoverishes, and contaminates him? Be sure of this: we are influencing people in one direction or the other by our manner of life. Our chief chance at greatness will be through influencing some other life to strive to live nobly—someone who, down the line, years later, turns out to be great partly because of us.

Christ said, "Let your light so shine before men that they may see your good works and give glory to your Father who is in heaven" (Matt. 5:16). *Indirect Greatness!* That's my second point.

3. Still again, Methuselah apparently received his niche in the hall of fame partly for carrying on a great tradition transmitted from the past.

Some people have the distinction of starting something great and others have the equally important distinction of carrying on something great that someone else began. If you will read the fourth chapter of Genesis you will find a list of the things which some of the early men on Cain's side of the human family accomplished. Cain himself had the distinction of committing the first murder: that was one way he got into the history books. He also had the honor of building the first walled city. Lamech had the questionable honor of starting polygamy. Jabal was the "father of those who dwell in tents and have cattle," that is, he was the first nomad. Jubal was the "father of those who play the harp and lyre," that is, he was the first musician. Tubalcain was "forger of all instruments of bronze and brass," that is, he was the first metalsmith. Another Lamech was the first person to compose a poem. Now Methuselah didn't start a thing. But he carried on something that somebody else started. And that is what the Book of Genesis from chapter 5 on, and the rest of the Bible from Genesis to Revelation, is all about.

We read in the last verse of chapter 4 of Genesis that religion —that is, the Hebrew religion—originated with Seth. In his day men first began to call upon the name of "the Lord" (Yahweh), the name for the Hebrew deity. So he is credited with having started the Hebrew religious tradition on its way—a religion which was different from, and more advanced than, any other ancient religion.

From that moment on, the historian lost all interest in Cain and the achievements of his offspring, and gave his entire attention to Seth and his offspring, and what happened to that tradition. A few generations pass and you read about Enoch, who "walked with God." Enoch was the father of Methuselah. Two more generations pass and you come to Noah. Still later you read about Abraham, Isaac, Jacob, Joseph, Saul, David, Solomon, the prophets—and finally Jesus. Methuselah was an important link in that long chain. He passed on the great tradition, which was the sole justification for recording the history of the Jews in the Bible, a history that unfolded step by step under the guidance of God and came to its culmination in Jesus and the early Christian church. From Seth to Jesus was a long time; nobody knows for certain how long. It well might have been several thousand years. But however long that period was, we can be sure it took that length of time for the Hebrew religion to become mature enough for God to bring it to its climax in Jesus, the Christ.

The early followers of the Master took his gospel out from Jerusalem, through Samaria and Asia Minor, across into Europe, from where in time, it moved into this continent of ours. Here in the United States we now have the accumulated results of two thousand years of costly, agonizing experimentation and experience, of trial and error procedure, of bitter contests of minds, of slow refining of Christian thinking. And how far have we come since the days of Jesus? Of course, we are only partly a Christianized people. Most of us Americans would say of ourselves what an Englishman is once reported to have said about himself: "Like most of my countrymen I am a heathen with Christian intervals." But how grateful we ought to be for the intervals.

Something immensely worthwhile for Christianity and for civilization has been achieved in this America of ours. All of it is closely related to, and in part, the fruitage of our Christian faith. We have not achieved this alone, but because of what countless others have accomplished, discovered, and transmitted from generation to generation since the days of Methuselah. We progress from age to age only to the extent that we stand culturally and otherwise on the shoulders of our predecessors and benefit from their cumulative achievements. Old truths become the matrix of new truths. It is the height of folly for any generation to throw away the accumulated wisdom, experience, and truth of past generations. Each new generation should begin where the last generation leaves off. It would be tragic for us, for the whole of mankind, and for God himself, if those of us who are guardians of the Christian faith in this country and in this century should fail to pass it on.

But you know, as well as I, that far too many of us Americans are indifferent to the best in our Western, semi-Christian society and are making little effort to conserve this and pass it on to the next generation in a stronger, more refined condition than that in which we received it. On the contrary, we are thoughtlessly ignoring or discarding it. It is nothing short of ominous how our freedoms, our Christian ideals, morals, ethics, and theistic beliefs are being thrown into the wastebasket by many American citizens in all walks of life.

In his poem "The Last Voyage" Alfred Noyes pictures a little girl, desperately ill, on a trans-Atlantic ship with no possibility of recovery unless she can have a certain delicate and difficult operation which can be performed only by a few specialists. By radio the captain of the ship learns that one of these specialists from Johns Hopkins Medical College is on another ship, within radio-phoning distance, going in the opposite direction. The ship physician gets in touch with the specialist, and tells his diagnosis, which is confirmed by the specialist. The specialist says, "If you will put on your earphones I can tell you step by step how to perform the operation." While the operation is going on two passengers on the deck are talking about it. One asks, "Do you think they'll save her?" The other replies, "They may save her. But who are they?" The man answers that not only will the two physicians be the saviors but the many people of many ages of the past who made both the radio and surgery possible must be counted saviors as well:

> Thousands of men, like cells
> In one organic brain, have worked together
> To make this moment possible, and evoke
> That one reply through darkness, to the call
> Our ship sent out tonight,
> And thousands more to guide our surgeon.

All of those people of the past are watching intently to see if the surgeon fails them. The human race is, in a sense, one organism: one generation achieves and transmits; the next receives, adds to it, and transmits again. All the past is watching to see how we make out—to see if we fail them. Numerous saints —reformers, prophets, ordinary Christians, our Master himself —all are watching to see what we do with the great heritage they passed on to us. If we fail, they fail. If we succeed, they succeed. That is what the author of the Book of Hebrews said in the great faith chapter, chapter 11, of his book. After picturing the heroes of the faith who labored without entering fully into the results of their own labors, he said that "apart from us they should not be made perfect" (11:30).

The question that each of us must ask himself pointedly is this: Am I going rashly to throw away the tested, tried, and proven truths of our Christian faith, so that they will have to be rediscovered at the loss of time and energy? Or am I going to hold to them, try to improve them, expand and refine them, and pass them on? I tell you, my friends, it is a great thing for any person to take hold of the past with one hand, and take hold of the future with the other and say, "This great religious tradition which began with Seth and culminated in Christ, shall pass through me." Each of us has a distinct and definite part to play in his brief lifetime, at his distinctive job, with his special God-given abilities, to be faithful in transmitting the great tradition. That is our chief chance at greatness.

Transmitted Greatness, greatness handed down as a legacy to future generations: that is my third point. (1) Behind-the-scenes greatness; (2) Indirect greatness; (3) Transmitted greatness.

III

Jesus gathered around Him a group of ordinary men and women—common folk for the most part. To them He committed the gospel, which is still the last best hope for a redeemed world. He said to them, "You are the light of the world . . . you are the salt of the earth." Those were the most solemn words, the most astounding words, He ever spoke: He entrusted the future of His kingdom to them.

According to a familiar legend, when Jesus returned to heaven, His work on earth finished, He was met by the Angel Gabriel, who asked Him what His plans were to make sure that His work would be carried on. Jesus replied, "I have given the message to Peter and John, to Mary and Martha. They will tell others and thus the message will spread." "But supposing," said the angel, "that the fishermen are too busy with their fishing, and the women with their housework, so that they forget to tell their friends or the friends forget to pass the message on. What other plans have you made, Lord?" Jesus paused, smiled a wonderful smile, and answered quietly, "I have no other plans. I am counting on them." Can He count on you? Can He count on me? Can He?

GIVE GOD TIME

We know that in everything God works for good with those who love him, who are called according to his purpose.
—ROMANS 8:28

I

SO FAR AS I am concerned Romans 8:28 is one of the golden texts of the Bible. I have quoted it oftener to myself than any other single text of Scripture, especially when I have been anxious or troubled, and I have commended it to others oftener than any other text when I have tried to counsel and comfort those in trouble.

This text is an illustration of illuminating changes in the meaning of a passage that sometimes result from the new translations of the Bible. The old King James Version reads: "We know that all things work together for good to them that love God, to them who are the called according to his purpose." The Revised Standard Version reads, "We *know* that *in* everything God works *for* good *with* those who *love* him, who are called according to *his purpose.*"

Paul does *not* say that all things are good or that if we love God and live according to his purposes everything will automatically and miraculously turn into good. He *does* say that, if we love God, believe in him, and give our lives to his purposes, he will work in everything with us to bring about what is good.

Why was Paul so sure of this? Because of his absolute certainty that in Christ God had revealed Himself fully—His nature, His character, His creative and redemptive purposes—to the human race. He believed, and this is made amply clear throughout his epistles, that the God who created and sustains the universe and everything in it, always was and always will be the kind of God revealed in Christ; or that God is—eternally is—a living Christ.

Hence Paul believed that God is personally in charge of the universe, not an absentee Creator who started the machinery in motion and then left it to operate itself thereafter. He said in his address at Athens, "God is not far from each of us, for in him we live and move and have our being" (Acts 17:27-28). A few verses before our text Paul makes the amazing statement that "the Spirit helps us in our weakness . . . intercedes for us with sighs too deep for words" (v. 26). This is equivalent to saying that God is emotionally involved in the human enterprise, that he identifies himself with us, suffers and struggles with us, pulls with us. That is exactly what the death of Christ meant to the early Christians.

Now read the text again. It implies that once something happens it becomes one more event to be incorporated into God's grand design for us, one more strand to be woven into His pattern for our lives, to be worked on by Him redemptively for our ultimate good. Until we give God time to work things out to their ultimate conclusions in His divine scheme for our lives, we cannot be sure whether they should be regarded as fortunate or unfortunate, good or bad. Hence, no matter what happens, don't give up or lose heart. Give God time!

II

If we make this our working faith we must first make sure that we really believe that God is actively involved with us in all phases of life: in the so-called natural order to which we belong, in the social order in which we live and work together, and in our individual lives.

1. God works with us in the natural order.

In our space age we are becoming more and more conscious of the solar system to which our planet Earth belongs. The space vehicles that are being launched into orbit remind us particularly of the law of gravitation, which, as one philosopher put it, "contains a problem of such dizzy vastness that our minds fail in the attempt to grasp it." If all the energy now available to our space scientists were multiplied many times and concentrated at one point it could not move the earth one inch into space. And yet gravitation sends it flying through space at many miles per minute. If gravitation suddenly failed, as the electricity in our homes does, the human race and the earth on which it lives would quickly disappear. We are vaguely aware, although we do not often stop to think about it, that our existence on this earth depends upon the rays of the sun, the effect of the moon on the earth, the cosmic rays from somewhere in outer space, the constant supply of water and of the chemical substance we call air and the many mysterious forces that keep the complex mechanisms in all living things continuously performing their jobs. Farmers, so it has been calculated, provide 5 percent of the energy necessary to produce crops, and nature's forces provide the other 95 percent. Our doctors know, but seldom mention, that they do not heal diseases but only assist the healing powers of nature to do their work.

For a number of years I have been making a file of articles clipped from the magazines to which I subscribe, articles that deal with the mysteries and wonders of life on the earth. One article describes the green leaf pigment called chlorophyll, the "one link between the sun and life, the conduit of perpetual energy to our own frail organisms. Every day, every hour of all the ages, chlorophyll ceaselessly creates—not figuratively but literally, in the grand First Chapter Genesis style. One instant there are a gas and water, as lifeless as the core of earth or the chill of space and the next they are become living tissue."

Other articles describe enzymes, cellular interrelations, genes,

and the "Inner Space" of living cells. Of the latter the writer
says, "Scientists are learning that the miniature world of the
single living cell is as astonishing as man himself. . . . When
future generations look back to our space age, they may well
regard the exploration of inner space—the depths of the living
cell—as far more important to humanity than the spectacular
achievements of the astronauts."

The wonders of the human body are dealt with by one group
of articles under such titles as "Your Amazing Circulatory System," "Our Amazing White Bloodstream," "The Chemical Wiz-
ard, Your Liver," "The Marvels of the Human Hand," "The
Lymphatic System," "Those Wonderful Windbags—Our Lungs,"
and "Your Body's Wizardry with Food." Of that last wonder the
writer says, "But for its brilliant chemical transformation, we
would starve. . . . It does in minutes jobs that would take hours
in the laboratory, or maybe could not be done at all." Still another article deals with "That Astounding Creator—Nature,"
which, "given virtually any environment will design a creature
for it, and some are almost unbelievable."

Do *you* attribute these wonders of nature to a Creator, spelled
with a capital "C"? Do you believe He is actively involved in,
at work in, all the forces—electrical, chemical, biological, and
so on, in the universe? If you were a doctor would you hang on
the walls of your office, as some physicians do, the saying attributed to the old physician Galen: "I dressed the wound and God
healed"? If you were a professor of chemistry would you stand
before a group of students in the laboratory where you were
about to begin an experiment and say, as Professor Joseph Henry
of Princeton University was accustomed, "Take off your hats;
I'm about to ask God a question"? If you were the head of a
team of scientists who are launching our space vehicles would
you, just before sending astronauts into space, breathe a silent
prayer saying, "God, we now entrust these astronauts to your
care. Your gravitation has never failed us yet, for which please
accept our profound, eternal gratitude"?

If these questions were addressed to me I would answer all of them in the affirmative without the slightest hesitation. If you could not do likewise it is doubtful whether you could join with Paul in saying, "We know that in everything [every natural thing] God works for good with those who love him."

But there is another side to nature's coin. There are times when nature appears to be working against us, not with us, when we have disasters such as earthquakes, volcanic eruptions, tidal waves, floods, tornadoes, and hurricanes. Perhaps it is this other side of nature that makes most of us wonder if God really is in charge of the universe, if He really seeks our good. Would Paul have included these things in the word "everything," in which he says God works with us for good? Yes, I think he would. His word "everything" seems to be all-inclusive.

There are many things in the world that we simply cannot understand at all, much less understand how they could possibly be permitted by a benevolent God. Although we now "see in a mirror dimly" and know "in part" (literally "in fragments"), as Paul put it (I Cor. 13:12), we do see good purpose in numerous places in the natural world. We take that as our clue to nature's Creator. The whole point of what Paul was saying is that we should believe that God is working with us in both the things we can understand and the things we cannot ferret out, in the things that are obviously for our welfare and the things that seem to do us harm, in the things that clearly are the deeds of love and things that appear to be unbecoming of a loving Father.

More specifically still, we have seen God in Christ and we believe Christ is the key to God's real nature. We believe that He loves us with an everlasting, immeasurable, never-failing love, with a love "that will not let us go." We are willing, therefore, to entrust ourselves to Him, to wait that love out to the end.

> In love and faith thy course of duty run.
> God nothing does, nor suffers to be done
> But thou would'st do the same
> Could thou but see the end of all events as he.

2. God works with us in the social order.

There are times when we are hard put to it to detect any meaning to history, to the movements and clashes of races, to the rise and fall of nations and civilizations. In the early chapters of Genesis God is pictured as being discouraged with His children, deciding to wipe them off the face of the earth and to start over again. Then follows the story of the flood. We fail to understand the meaning of that old story if we do not observe that God couldn't consent to destroy the race completely, and that immediately after the flood He started to work with them anew. That is what the Bible from that point on means, namely, God's unwillingness to give the race up and His determination to work with it until His divine purposes for it are achieved.

As difficult as it is to do so, students of history claim to be able to see that "through the ages one increasing purpose runs." Interestingly enough the men who have been most actively engaged in making history—those out in the arena fighting for an improved world—are the ones who are likeliest to find evidences of "a power not ourselves making for righteousness."

In his study of the Battle of Waterloo, Victor Hugo said that it was not possible for Napoleon to have won, because he had been impeached before the infinite and his fall decreed. "He vexed God," Hugo said. "Waterloo is not a battle; it is the change of front of the universe."

Oliver Cromwell once spoke of "strange windings and turnings of Providence" that cross and thwart the purposes of men in their military compaigns. Winston Churchill once said that when a war starts it looks like science but by the time it ends it looks more like astrology, that is to say, the outcome of the great wars of history are often determined by what appears to be trivial events, not by the heaviest armaments and the most skilled leaders. Lincoln said, "I hold myself as an instrument of Providence." During the distressing days of the First World War, President Woodrow Wilson told his personal secretary that he would go crazy if he did not believe in the providence of God.

It is almost axiomatic with many of our greatest scholars that a development takes place in history which cannot be attributed to the expressed purposes of the men most involved in it. Bergson, the French philosopher, said that there is in history the constant recurrence of a "persistent Something" that keeps reasserting itself. He called this "elan vital," the vital impulse, the soul of the universe. The Old Testament prophets called this the direct hand of God in human affairs. Hence in the Old Testament we find such statements as these: ". . . The race is not to the swift nor the battle to the strong . . ." (Eccl. 9:11); ". . . Not by might, nor by power, but by my Spirit, says the Lord of Hosts" (Zech. 4:6).

It is fitting that the New Testament should end with the Book of Revelation. For it was addressed to the early Christians by John, at a time when the Roman Empire was trying, apparently with success, to destroy Christianity. Just when things looked the darkest John assured them that God is not dead, but alive and at work, that evil is doomed, that Rome will fall, that righteousness will conquer and that the Kingdom of God will be established on the earth.

If one is able to say with Paul, "I know that in everything God works for good with those who love him," he must believe, despite all evidence to the contrary, that history does have meaning, that it is moving, even though circuitously and unevenly, toward divine ends.

3. God works with us in our individual lives.

Now and then someone says, "What do you ministers mean when you say that God works 'in' us?" We mean what many successful men have meant when they have said that the powers they used in their particular callings were not resident *in* them but working *through* them, that they did not carve out their own careers themselves but were divinely led into and through them. You find this sort of attitude being expressed by men in all fields of endeavor: musicians, artists, poets, scientists, inventors, statesmen, and businessmen.

Graham Taylor, a noted religious leader of the early part of this century, said, "I did not devise my way: I discerned it." Shakespeare made Hamlet observe, "There's a divinity that shapes our ends, rough hew them how we will." The first message Morse sent through his newly invented telegraph instrument was, "What hath God wrought?" When Haydn completed his *Creation,* he gave God all the credit. Robert Louis Stevenson humbly confessed, "It is with gratitude and wonder that I consider the way in which I have been led." Elizabeth Barrett Browning stated this feeling, so commonly expressed by others, thus:

> The best men doing their best
> Know peradventure least of what they do.
> Men usefullest in the world are simply used.

When we say that God works in us, we also refer to the experiences of many people who have been stricken with misfortune. They are able to face their misfortunes with courage and even turn them into blessings because of the inner resources which come to them—resources that they do not possess and could not generate by their own efforts.

Some publisher should put out a series of brief biographical sketches that deal successively with celebrated people who have overcome the handicaps of deafness, blindness, paralysis, stuttering, congenital defects, poverty, general ill-health, and accidents. It sometimes looks as if the first step toward success is a handicap of some description. Franklin D. Roosevelt is an outstanding recent illustration of this. Those who have written about him agree that his attack of polio was the turning point in his career. From that he emerged a different man, with a mellower spirit and a deeper philosophy. When Beethoven realized that he was becoming deaf, he thought it was the worst calamity that could possibly happen to him—that it was, in fact, the end of his musical career. Then one day he said, "I will seize Fate by the throat; most assuredly it shall not get me wholly down." In spite of his deafness—perhaps partly because of it—he wrote such music that one of his biographers said, "We are eternal debtors to his deafness."

I do not say that all handicapped people have attributed their courage directly to God. But many of them have done so—a very large proportion of them, in fact. And thousands of others who have faced other types of misfortunes, such as business reverses, unexpected and tragic deaths in the family, long illnesses, and the like, have openly done the same thing.

The ancient cynic who wrote the book of Ecclesiastes said, "This is an evil in all that is done under the sun that one fate comes to all . . ." (9:3). The same things do happen to us all alike. But all people do not take them alike. And that makes all the difference in the world with the outcome of events. "The worst turns to the best when met by the brave." Resources are available to a Christian that can make him brave, that will enable him like Paul to demonstrate to the world that he can do all things in Christ who strengthens him. (Cf. Phil. 4:13.)

III

I say again, whatever happens—in the natural world, in the social order, in your individual life—even if you think it is the worst possible misfortune, don't get discouraged, don't give up, but wait, work, pray, trust, and give God time. In everything — literally everything—God works with us to bring about good. Nothing is final until God gets through working on it with his redemptive love. Such is our amazing, our marvelous Christian faith.

A MAN SURPRISED AT HIMSELF

"Is it I, Lord?"

—Matthew 26:22

I

WHILE JESUS WAS having intimate fellowship with his twelve disciples at their last supper, he said to them, "Truly, I say to you, one of you will betray me." Whereupon they were very sorrowful and began to say to him one after another, "Is it I, Lord?" *All* of them asked the same question.

Wasn't that strange? Didn't they know what they were going to do? The point of the biblical story is that they did not know. Sufficient information is given about two of the twelve—Peter and Judas—to indicate that this is what the story intends to imply.

Peter later declared, "Though they all fall away because of you, I will never fall away. . . . Even if I must die with you, I will not deny you." But shortly thereafter, he did what he vowed he would never do—what he never intended to do. He was surprised at the possibility for evil in himself. On the other hand, Judas deliberately plotted to destroy Jesus, to betray him for money. He had it all neatly planned and worked out to the last detail. Then he found that he couldn't go through with it. He was surprised at the possibility for good in himself.

86

The more we learn about human beings—including ourselves
—the more we are surprised by the capacities for evil in us, on
the one hand, and on the other hand, by the capacities for good.
Emerson said, "Every man is a divinity in disguise, a god playing
the fool." A god . . . and a fool . . . side by side in the same
person! We know why he said that. All of us have our high
moments of exaltation, insight, and inspiration, which make us
feel like sons of God—and our low moments of depression, moral
failure, selfish desires, and unworthy deeds which make us feel
like children of Satan. Now with Goethe we cry, "Great God!
What a thing is the heart of man!". . . . "Much there is that is
weird, but naught is weirder than man." Then with Hamlet we
say, "What a piece of work is man! How noble in reason! How
infinite in faculty. . . . In action how like an angel, in apprehen-
sion how like a god!" Surprised—now at the divine, now at the
devilish within us.

II

1. A man surprised at the evil in himself.

Peter asked, "Is it I? Am I going to betray you?" Jesus said,
"Yes, and more than once—three times." Peter declared, "I
will never, never, never do that." Yet within a few brief hours
he had not only done what he said he would not do, but had
done it vehemently, with great vigor, with profanity—in fact,
like a mad man. I have no doubt that he afterward said to himself, "How could I have done this dastardly thing? What happened to me? Did I lose my mind? Was I possessed? It must
have been a demon. I—*I* really didn't do it!"

No man is safe until he recognizes the abysmal possibilities
for evil in himself and deals with that fact realistically, courageously, vigorously, continuously.

The capacity for evil in us has its roots, of course, in the fact
that God made us free moral agents. He took a great risk when
He made us complicated personalities, with all sorts of contra-
dictory forces wrapped up in the same bundle, and endowed us

with the responsibility and power of direction and freedom to use those forces, instead of making us automatons. The responsibilities of freedom are fraught with danger. To exercise that freedom, to learn how to exercise it wisely and well, is our chance of becoming the sons of God. And that is precisely what we are here on earth for—why we are entrusted with life itself.

Every person needs to take a good, hard look—to keep on taking a good, hard look—at the potential evil that he can do to himself and to others. Not in a morbid way, and not with self-depreciation and condemnation, but with alertness and awareness of the dangerous, damaging evil of which he is capable. Continuously throughout the whole of life he must remember that he is never morally safe, never sure that his mind or his emotions will not play tricks upon him. The things he means to do and the things he wants to do, he may not do; and the things he does *not* want or mean to do he may do, as Paul discovered again and again (Romans 7), *unless*—that is a *very* important "unless." It is fraught with destiny. *Unless he arms himself against himself.*

And how does he do that? One arms himself with principles, convictions, purposes, ideals, standards, obligations, and disciplines. There are numerous signs that our generation is afraid of those words, trying to avoid them and evade them and eliminate them altogether from our theological vocabulary. There is an open aversion, even hostility, to moral standards of all descriptions nowadays among many groups. We are told that a person with moral standards is a moralist, or a legalist; that a person engaged in spiritual or religious disciplines is exhibiting piosity or self-righteousness, or is guilty of negativism, puritanism, and the like.

And yet, one of the functions of Jesus is continually to bring us face to face with our possible sinful selves. He probes deep. He goes beyond the deed to the motive: not murder but hate, not adultery but lust, not words but thoughts—sins of attitude, of temperament, of disposition, of omission as well as of commission. He extended, broadened, and deepened the concept of sin.

On the one hand, He urged His followers to make a manly moral effort to root out those things which trick and trap us. He warned against temporizing, trifling, self-deception, wishful thinking. He compared the struggle of life to a radical surgical operation: pluck out the eye, cut off the hand if these offend you, He said. On the other hand, He asked for complete dedication, consecration, and commitment of the self—of body, of instinct, of emotions and mind, of will, of talents, of money. This complete dedication sublimates the inner forces of our lives and channels them in the right direction.

Recently I read through the New Testament hurriedly for the sole purpose of making a list of the words and expressions which are used to indicate the part every man plays in his own religious disciplines and growth. They are numerous. Here are just a few of them: "Shun . . . Aim at . . . Contend . . . Having done all stand . . . Set your minds . . . Resist . . . Be perfect . . . Be sober . . . Be watchful . . . Never flag . . . Earnestly desire . . . Press on . . . Think on these things . . . Put to death . . . Practice these duties . . . Train yourself in godliness . . . Devote yourself . . . Do your best to . . . Be steady . . . Gird up your minds . . . Make every effort to . . . Be the more zealous to . . . Put away . . . Put on . . . Put off . . . Fight the good fight . . . Be strong . . . Be courageous . . . Ask . . . Seek . . . Knock . . . ." Paul sums it up thus: ". . . Work out your own salvation with fear and trembling, for God is at work in you, both to will and to work, for his good pleasure" (Phil. 2:12-13). We give God His chance to work in us, with us, through us, by exercising eternal vigilance on our part, by putting forth our maximum effort. Our moral struggles are our response to the forgiving love of God, our gratitude for his unmerited grace. His redeeming love calls forth our best endeavors. The two things—*grace and moral effort*—belong together, and what God hath joined together, let no man put asunder.

There is no such thing as a Christian life devoid of moral and spiritual effort. *Let that be said! Make note of that in the deep recesses of your soul! Etch it indelibly on your mind!* In the battle of life we must put on the whole armor of God—all the moral weapons, both offensive and defensive, at our disposal; all the spiritual disciplines, private and public, individual and corporate, which have been part and parcel of our religion from the very beginning. *That, and only that* is our safeguard against the surprise attacks of evil.

Upon reflection, upon a good look at ourselves, does it not seem clear that what happened to Peter is no mystery? We can think of several varied explanations of his weakness. He left some unguarded place, some untamed force, some unresolved conflict, some hangover from his careless youth, something lurking in his heart, unpurged, gnawing, instead of trying to root it out. Or, he neglected his positive spiritual disciplines, the cultivation of strong, healthy, inner habits which strengthened his moral fibre. *He failed somewhere in his moral and spiritual disciplines.* He may have had the best of good intentions, but he didn't carry through. Manifestly, he had not built up within him those deep-seated convictions that carry the weight of our intentions. He was not fortified against the instinct of self-preservation inside nor against group pressures from outside. In short, *he failed to face the realistic fact of the potential evil in himself.*

To his credit, be it said that when he realized what had happened he wept bitterly—tears not only of regret and remorse but of genuine repentance. And he started all over again on his struggle. We know from the facts given of his later life that this time he made the grade.

2. A man surprised at the good in himself.

It may sound strange that I would say that Judas was surprised at the good in himself. Ordinarily his question, "Is it I who will betray you, Lord?" is thought of as a hypocritical remark to hide his real intentions. But the facts in the record do not support that interpretation. Explain his motives as you will—and many reasons for his actions have been offered—the record reveals that he had a hard, almost successful fight with himself. He plotted the betrayal deliberately. Apparently he could have succeeded with his plan without any outward ill effects. But he found to his surprise that he could not go through with it. No one tried to stop him. Apparently no one but Jesus knew about it at the time. Something within his own heart stopped him. He found out that he was a better man—potentially a better man—than he had supposed.

If we could see that whole event dramatically portrayed on the stage, I am sure that at the moment of his offering back the money, the audience would burst into spontaneous applause. A modern artist has tried to depict the scene on canvas. Judas, fully aware of what he has done, is stricken with remorse. The thirty pieces of silver burned his hands. He rushed back, panting, into the presence of the priests who had bribed him. The veins and cords of his neck are taut and swollen. His mouth is open for breath as well as for speech. His eyes are bulging, his cheeks haggard. He is clutching the neck of the empty sack with one hand and offering the money back with the other. The handle of a knife extends from his girdle to suggest the contemplation of a desperate act. As he offers to return the money he is saying, "I have betrayed innocent blood!" I think the artist has success-fully interpreted the inner struggle the man was having with himself. He made no excuses. He didn't lay the blame on any-body else. He did not rationalize. He pleaded no extenuating circumstances. He looked for no scapegoat. He sought no avenue of escape from his personal responsibility. He made an honest confession. He took the blame. With utter candor he faced the bald fact about himself. "I have betrayed innocent blood!" he cried. That was an honorable, a courageous thing to do, and a desperately difficult thing to do. We feel almost instinctively even when we read the biblical account, "He's about to make a come-back! He's going to crash through! He's on the way to redemp-tion!" And then he went out. . . . A period of time elapsed—a few hours, a day, three days, no one knows how long. Apparently he shunned company. He sought no forgiveness. Unlike Peter, he shed no tears. Evidently he brooded. He utterly condemned him-self. And then—he committed suicide.

Precisely what was his difficulty? The good impulse, the honest impulse, within him was clamoring for a hearing. God was confronting him in the innermost citadel of his soul. He refused to believe that there was forgiveness for him, or that he could come back, or that he had another chance. This was his great mistake, his great sin—not to heed the call of the best in him, not to listen to the voice of God at that moment. Adelaide Love has said that the sin of Judas, his unutterable sin, the greatest wrong man can commit, was

> To doubt the essence of God's fatherhood,
> The inexhaustible and infinite
> Capacity of Godhead to forgive.

I call upon myself and upon each of you to face that man's tragic condition. We cannot understand man, I said earlier, without recognizing his capacity for sin. Now I say, neither can we understand man without recognizing his capacity for good, for godlikeness. At the heart of our Christian faith is the belief that men are made in the image of God, that all men have something akin to God in them—"a spark of divinity," if you wish to call it that. "Man's unhappiness," said Thomas Carlyle, "comes from his greatness. It is because there is an infinite in him, which, with all his cunning, he cannot quite bury under the finite."

When we think we are through with God; when we suppose we have dismissed Him and turn to purely human, mere mundane physical, earthly things; even when we think we are planning evil, something hostile to what we suppose religion and religious folks to be—God is there! "What you are doing, you are doing unto me. . . . What you are not doing, you are not doing to me," Jesus said. "I have girded you, although you didn't know it," said Isaiah to Cyrus. In an unexpected moment of some sort, there comes a tinge of pity, a flash of insight, a strange affection, a recognition of truth or beauty, a smiting of conscience—*God is there!* He is there—longing, waiting, hoping, ready to forgive.

H. L. Mencken, the clever critic and cynic, who died some

years ago, who was known well to the sophisticated of another
generation, said more than once that he had never had a religious
impulse in his life; that he didn't believe in God. But hardly an
issue of the *American Mercury,* of which he was editor, was
printed in which he did not lambaste, sarcastically criticise religion in some manner, bitterly attack religious people, or scoff
at their cherished beliefs. He simply couldn't leave religion alone.
Why? I believe there was something within him akin to God
that he did not have the courage, or the good sense, to give a
chance to express itself. Many of the authors of the novels, plays,
essays, etc., that are now so popular with a great many of the
intellectuals who are occupying the center of the stage on the
present American scene, are, if I am any judge, like Mencken.
They cannot leave religion alone. They are angry, bitter, cynical,
scoffing—yet they cannot keep from making passing and occasional incisive references to God or to the Bible. They cannot, so
to speak, keep from tipping their hats to God, from making a
friendly gesture to God—all of which reveals their inner spiritual
needs, if not their secret unconscious and unsatisfied spiritual
hunger. The core of their predicament is their unwillingness to
give the occasional sparks of godliness and goodness, the tinges
and touches of the Spirit of God in their souls, a chance to glow
and grow.

The wardens of our large prisons tell us that hardened criminals
will often risk their lives to save a fellow prisoner or quickly
volunteer to become guinea pigs for testing some new drug, and
that they are generous to a fault. These things simply show what
they might have been if only they had given that "something"
inside them its optimum opportunity.

> Down in the human heart, crushed by the tempter,
> Feelings lie buried that grace can restore.
> Touched by a loving heart, wakened by kindness,
> Chords that were broken, can vibrate once more.

I said earlier that one major function of Jesus is to reveal to us our capacity for sin. Now I say that another of His main functions is to reveal our best selves, our possible selves, to us. Something in us, long suppressed or sleeping, unexplored, unstirred, unexploited, pleads with us to give it a chance. He reminds us again and again that potentially we are all sons of God, of infinite worth in the eyes of God—worth redeeming, and, thanks be to Him, redeemable. *He keeps us sensitized to God!*

No man will ever know what he really is or can become until God takes hold of his life and he takes hold of God. "Oh, for a man to arise in me that the man I am may cease to be," someone once said. That's possible! Fan that flicker of goodness and greatness in your heart to flame! One of the noblest utterances of Nietzsche was, "I charge thee, throw not away the hero in thy soul." Don't let your soul's noblest potentiality go to waste. Give God a chance to release "the imprisoned splendour in your soul."

Can Christ who "called the unknown best from Peter, James and all the rest" until He "drew forth their deepest selves"—can He again do that for us? Yes, He can! Shout that abroad! Never forget that! Never let others forget it! Never leave that out of Christian preaching, Christian teaching, Christian evangelism!

III

Our whole human life is a battle between God and Satan for possession of our souls. If a man would be heroic, he must welcome that conflict with enthusiasm. That is the price he pays for his own soul—the way he vindicates God's wisdom in making him a free person.

When the fight begins within himself
A man's worth something. God stoops o'er his head,
Satan looks up between his feet—both tug—
He's left, himself i' the middle: the soul wakes
and grows.

ROBERT BROWNING

The soul of man is one of the decisive battlefields—*the* decisive battlefield—of the world. Fully aware of this fundamental fact, the Apostle Paul urged the young man Timothy to "fight the good fight of the faith . . ." (I Tim. 6:12); exhorted the members of the early Christian church to "be watchful, to stand firm in your faith, to be courageous and strong" (I Cor. 16:13); assured them that he was continually praying that "God would grant them to be strengthened with might through the Spirit in the inner man"; and promised them that "the power at work within them is able to do far more abundantly than all that they ask or think" (cf. Eph. 3:16-21). In the name of Paul's Lord and ours I lay upon you the same exhortations, offer you the same assurances, and make you the same promises.

POLICING OURSELVES

. . . You are not under law but under grace.

—ROMANS 6:14

I

S OMEONE WAS recently quoted as having said, "The future of our country depends upon whether we can take the policeman off the street corner and put him in our hearts." The person who said that unwittingly expressed one of the central doctrines of our Christian faith, the doctrine of grace.

The genius of our Christian religion is this: Its followers are supposed to have an inner motive and power that compels them voluntarily to love, to be just, to live righteously. This was set forth by the Apostle Paul in the 6th chapter of his letter to the Romans. In this chapter he explains that the Christian's acceptance of Christ by faith is a vital union with Him, in which, so to speak, the believer experiences the events through which Christ passed in his death, burial, and resurrection. These events are typified in a Christian's baptism, in which symbolically he descends into, is buried under, and ascends out of the water. Hence, Paul says, Christians are to think of themselves as ". . . dead to sin and alive to God in Christ Jesus" (Rom. 6:11). Once they have gone through this transforming experience they are expected to live like transformed people. Paul exhorts his readers, "Let not

96

sin therefore reign in your mortal bodies. . . . Do not yield your members to sin as instruments of wickedness, but yield yourselves to God as men who have been brought from death to life, and your members to God as instruments of righteousness. For sin will have no dominion over you, since you are not under law but under grace" (Rom. 6:12-14).

The word "grace" is unquestionably the most significant single word in the Bible. It is our English word for Hebrew and Greek words that indicate the nature of God out of which proceed his gracious acts of the creation, the preservation, and the redemption of his children. Always these acts grow out of his unmerited love. As soon as a person experiences that grace, it has the singular effect of making him want to be gracious to his fellowmen, to manifest toward others the kind of love God manifests toward him. Out of sheer gratitude to God for his redeeming love in Christ, the Christian is compelled, not by outside pressures but voluntarily, from within the citadel of his being, to be loving, just and fair. Such is the Christian doctrine of grace.

Let us look at some of the implications of this doctrine.

II

1. The strength of any society depends not upon the number of its laws but upon the number of its citizens who do right voluntarily.

Dr. Martin Luther King said to a group of students attending a conference in late December, 1967: "Maybe the law cannot change the heart, but it can restrain the heartless. Perhaps law cannot legislate morals, but law can regulate behavior. It may be that law can't make a man love me, but it can restrain him from lynching me." He was right, of course. He might have said even more. Law can perform other useful functions, chief of which is to be the spearhead of needed social education.

I remember quite distinctly when a law was first passed to make it a criminal offense to use phosphorus in the manufacture of matches. This law was passed because it had been discovered that the dread disease which afflicted numerous people and which later was to become known as "phossy jaw" was directly attributable to the phosphorus handled by the workers making the matches. I also remember when it first became widely known that a cow's milk could carry tuberculosis germs and infect those who drink it. So laws were passed requiring that dairy herds be given tests and vaccinated to prevent the spread of tuberculosis. Other laws have been passed to control such matters as building codes, installation of plumbing, the conditions under which foods and drugs are produced and processed, working conditions in factories—all of which were designed to safeguard public health.

Legislation has been at least partly responsible for eliminating such social wrongs as child labor and human slavery. Let us hope that before long we will look back upon the troubled years through which we are now passing and say, "The agony involved in legislating about civil rights aided in ending another wrong."

But laws have their limitations. As Dr. King intimated, they are not intended to make people good, or to make them love one another, but only to restrain them from harming others. In themselves laws are not the basis of our security nor the measure of our stability as a nation.

Some years after the First World War Lord Moulton, Britain's minister of munitions in that war, made an address in which he used a phrase, "Obedience to the unenforceable," which has been widely referred to ever since. He explained that his phrase applied to those citizens who voluntarily obey laws which no outsider could possibly force them to obey. He went on to express the belief that the real greatness of a nation—its true civilization—is measured by the number of citizens who enforce laws upon themselves.

Upon reflection I am sure that most of us would agree that our country's strength is to be measured not by the number of its laws, but by the number of its citizens who need no laws. And yet, there are times when it appears that we Americans are putting our faith in laws rather than in the quality of our citizens.

At least far too many of us in recent years have been putting the larger share of our energies on pressing for better legislation rather than on striving to make better men.

It has been estimated that at the present time in our country a complete law library would require 5,500 volumes of statutes and 180,000 volumes of interpretation of statutes by the courts. The person making the estimate said that if we continue to pass laws in the next hundred years at the same rate we have passed them in the last hundred years, a century hence a complete law library will require 500,000 volumes of statutes and 1,800,000 volumes of interpretations of statutes. With that vast number of laws to guide us we Americans presumably would be a law-abiding people. Actually we are rapidly becoming a lawless people, and on all hands there are demands and pressures for more laws and for more governmental inspectors, investigators, and enforcement officials to make it harder to evade laws without being caught.

It is a sad commentary upon the moral state of our country that we have to be compelled by law to treat one another justly. The very fact that so many laws seem necessary indicates that something is badly awry in our citizens.

The headmaster of Eton, the famous boys' school in England, once said in a chapel talk to the boys, "It is your duty to be pure in heart, and if you are not I shall flog you." As if anyone could make a boy pure in heart by punishing him. One might prevent him from committing an impure act by keeping an eye on him all the time. But the moment he is in no danger of being caught, he will do what his heart prompts him to do.

In a striking editorial in the religious journal *The Christian Century* the editor discussed the alarming number of deaths in automobile accidents in our land, and concluded that the best thing to save the lives of the drivers of automobiles who, statistically speaking, are sure to die in the next year, is for the church to find a way to speak to their condition: "That condition is that of a man driving a machine that is running wild because it lacks a spiritual governor."

The safety of our country does not lie in our laws nor in our law enforcement officials, as important as these are. It lies rather where Lord Moulton said it lies, in the number of our citizens who need no laws to force them to think of the welfare of their fellowmen but who force themselves to do this.

2. The number of citizens in our society who do right voluntarily depends upon how many of them are religiously motivated.

Our Lord was charged with being opposed to the Hebrew system of law. In dealing with this charge in one section of the Sermon on the Mount (Matt. 5) He declared that He came not to abolish the law but to fulfill it. Having said that, He set forth a higher form of righteousness that He expected of His followers— a righteousness that exceeds, or goes beyond, the righteousness of the scribes and Pharisees, and that strikes deeper than the law because it goes beyond the deed to the motives and the thoughts of the heart. Later He stated that both the law and the prophets of Israel may be summarized in two commandments: to love God with all one's heart, soul, and mind, and to love his neighbor as himself (Matt. 23:36f). Jesus did not lay down rules for His followers but sought followers who would impose rules on themselves. He did not try to coerce the wills or compel the devotion of people. He invited them to follow Him cheerfully of their own free will. In short, He summoned them to a voluntary righteousness that is generated by the expulsive and the compulsive power of a great affection.

We commonly speak of one of Jesus' sayings as "The Golden Rule," which is not a legalistic rule at all but another way of stating what he said at other times about loving one's neighbors. "So whatever you wish that men would do to you, do so to them; for this is the law and the prophets" (Matt. 7:12). How often we have repeated that—and heard others repeat it—saying, "That is my religion." But I wonder! I wonder if we have understood what we were saying. That utterance has far more significance than most of us ordinarily suppose. "You want to know how to treat your fellow men?" Jesus implies. "Then use your imagination: put yourself in the other person's place and treat him as you would want to be treated under the same conditions. Before you are told to do it, or a law is passed to try to force you to do it, voluntarily, on your own initiative—even before a person knows you have thought of him—treat him as you would like to be treated." That is called using Christian imagination. That tremendous force created the early Christian Church —what someone has called "a fellowship of holy imagination." Is there anything more badly needed everywhere than that? Suppose we treated the other person, his life, his property, his reputation, his problems, his needs and desires, with creative imagination? How would you like to be treated, for example, if you were working at the other person's job, practicing his profession, living in his situation, carrying his responsibilities, a member of his social or racial group? Well, use your Christian imagination and do some creative and constructive thinking about him. Do this voluntarily, on your own, because you want to do it, because to satisfy the promptings of your heart you must do it. That is what the Golden Rule really means.

Dr. Ralph W. Sockman says, "It is one thing to care enough for oneself to refrain from doing harm to others; it is quite another thing to care enough for others to have a passion for doing him good. It is the part of a gentleman to be decent with a distaste for unrighteousness. It is a mark of a Christian to hunger and thirst after righteousness." Love anticipates another's desires, welfare, needs, happiness.

The Apostle Paul set forth this same general teaching in his letter to the Romans (ch. 13). He was faced with the same charge as Jesus had been, that Christians were against laws. Paul declared that Christians are not against laws as such, but rather they are bound by another and higher law, thus repeating what Jesus himself had made clear, that Christians are under a new, more significant, more inclusive law—the law of love. Paul put the matter this way: "Owe no one anything, except to love one another; for he who loves his neighbor has fulfilled the law. Love does no wrong to a neighbor; therefore love is the fulfilling of the law" (13:8, 10).

Under the leadership of its mayor, San Francisco carried on a campaign sometime ago designed to reduce the number of deaths of pedestrians in traffic accidents. In a statement to the public the mayor said, "Any driver of a car who has any of the instincts of a gentleman would recognize the rights of a pedestrian when the pedestrian has the right of way. Automobile drivers must be taught to develop a sense of responsibility, a greater consideration of other drivers and of pedestrians." Change one word in a phrase of that statement to read, "Any driver of a car who has any of the instincts of a Christian," etc. An instinct is something innate, born in us, that operates almost spontaneously. A Christian has instincts, or should have, that are a part of his second nature—born in him when he himself is born anew. Almost automatically because it is his nature to do so, his desire to do so, his sense of responsibility, he seeks the welfare of others, treats them fairly.

3. The number of religiously motivated citizens in our society depends, so far as Christianity is concerned, upon whether the church is doing its divinely appointed work effectually.

Whether we church folk like it or not, we cannot escape the fact that organized society as a whole regards the church as the institution par excellence for equipping people with the inner qualities for good citizenship. Church members should also regard this as their primary role in society and welcome the challenge this offers to a rebirth of zeal for their faith, to exhibit holy boldness to propagate it, in particular to persuade themselves and others to discover the inner resources it offers for brotherly group living.

One great trouble at present is that so many Christian ministers, especially when dealing with young people, seem to be more eager to acquaint people with statistical surveys and sociological studies of human behavior than to acquaint them with the part the Chris-

tian religion can play in practical, responsible Christian citizenship.

A recent news item in the religious press typifies this attitude.
The item quoted from a statement made by the dean of the
chapel of an Eastern university concerning the prevalence of
cheating among students. He estimated that from 40 to 60 percent of college students cheat, some more and some less. He gave
three reasons for their cheating: (1) to outwit the professor and
beat the system where grades count too much; (2) to please
overly ambitious parents; and (3) to get a little practice on how
they are going to have to live in a highly competitive society after
they graduate. Nothing was said in the news dispatch about the
dean's censuring students for their dishonesty, or attributing it
to a deficiency in the quality of either their religion or of their
moral character, or exhorting them to live up to the potentialities
and obligations of their faith. The school's grading system, the
parents, and society were blamed—not the students.

The moral condition of our Western civilization demands some
straight thinking and some equally straight speaking. We are
deceiving ourselves if we imagine that our modern scientific age
is on the verge of discovering some novel and easy way to change
the moral behavior of the human race. It simply is not going to
be done. The only way radically to modify the conduct of people
is by the time-honored method of changing their hearts. It has
never been possible and will never be possible to maintain a high
quality of moral and ethical living without spiritual means—
without developing within people a sense of obligation to their
Maker, a desire and determination to live up to His divine intentions and expectations for them, a set of high aims and ideals,
a willingness to assume some responsibilities for themselves and to
engage in the spiritual and moral disciplines by which men have
always generated the resources for their upward striving. The
heart is the clue to better men, and the clue to the heart is the
grace of God.

It is high time that we Christians begin to say these things
without apology and without embarrassment—without mincing

words, engaging in hairsplitting arguments over theological and philosophical semantics, halting and hedging and beating around the bush, pussyfooting, searching for some type of scapegoat on which to lay the blame for our weakness.

III

Hawthorne tells a strange tale, "Earth's Holocaust," about a time when the inhabitants of earth, "overburdened with an accumulation of wornout trumpery, determined to rid themselves of it by a general bonfire." All night long a stranger with cynical smile and haughty air stood in the background, watching them bring things which they considered evil—trashy books, implements of war, liquor, tobacco, and what not—and toss them into the fire. Late in the night the stranger approached and said, "There is one thing that these wiseacres have forgotten to throw into the fire, and without which all the rest of the conflagration is just nothing at all—yes, though they have burnt the earth itself to cinders." "And what may that be?" someone asked. He replied, "What but the human heart itself; and unless they hit upon some method of purifying that foul cavern, forth from it will reissue all the shapes, or worse ones, which they have taken such a vast deal of trouble to consume to ashes. . . . Oh, take my word for it, it will be the old world yet."

We Christians have been entrusted with the spiritual means for cultivating the heart—the gospel of God's redeeming grace in Christ. That gospel is our "hope" for a brotherly world. To proclaim and explain the gospel with never-flagging zeal; to bring increasingly all known powers of persuasion to bear upon the minds, the consciences, the wills and the judgments of men to accept God's proffered grace, to yield themselves to the power of the gospel and live by it, and under its inspiration to consecrate themselves and their abilities to the job of transforming the earth into God's Great Society—this is the Church's fundamental work in the world. All its energies, resources, and organizational machinery should be continuously devoted toward the effectual performance of this task.

Yes, the man who said, "The future of our country depends upon whether we can take the policeman off the street corner and put him in our hearts," spoke more wisely than he knew. The heart is the monitor of our souls, or, to change the figure, the mainspring of our lives. The ancient wise man urged the youth of his day, "Keep your heart with all vigilance, for from it flow the springs of life" (Prov. 4:23). That is sound advice for all ages of people in every period of history.

THE RESPONSIBLE PERSON

So Joseph said to his brothers, "Come near to me, I pray you." And they came near. And he said, 'I am your brother, Joseph, whom you sold into Egypt. And now do not be distressed, or angry with yourselves, because you sold me here; for God sent me before you to preserve life."

—GENESIS 45:4-5

I

THE STORY OF Joseph and his brothers is widely recognized as one of the world's great short stories. Thomas Mann, the German author, thought so much of its literary worth and possibilities that he used it as the basis of a four-volume work of fiction entitled *Joseph and His Brethren*. If the story were the product of someone's imagination, its author would deserve a high rank among the writers of fiction. But if it actually happened, as seems certain, the reporter who told it deserves high praise for his literary skill in showing that truth is not only stranger than fiction but can be more fascinating. He deserves our thanks for succeeding so admirably in picturing Joseph as a conspicuous example of the responsible, dependable person.

II

1. Joseph's early life.

Joseph was next to the youngest son in a family of twelve boys. The story of his life revolves around the hostility of his brothers toward him. Apparently there were five reasons for this hostility.

(1) It was the by-product of a polygamous household. His

106

father, Jacob, was married to four women—two wives and two concubines. The mothers were jealous of one another and for their children and were constantly competing for the favors of their husband. Hostilities between children can develop in the best of monogamous families, but in the atmosphere of Jacob's family they were almost certain to appear.

(2) Joseph was the child of his father's old age. Jacob became overindulgent and lenient with his younger boys. That is the natural inference from the historian's statement that Jacob "loved Joseph more than any other of his children because he was the son of his old age." In any family of several children, older children are likely to say to their father, "You were stricter with us than you are with the younger children. You let them do as they please. They can get by with anything." Whenever and wherever this feeling arises it can build up into an explosive situation.

(3) He was his father's favorite. After stating that Jacob loved Joseph more than his other children the writer adds, "And he made him a long robe with sleeves." The scholars believe this robe was a garment such as worn by persons of distinction. When Joseph wore it he stood out as a little prince among commoners, so to speak. Joseph was the first of two children by Jacob's favorite wife, Rachel, the only one of the four women he truly loved. Even down to his old age Jacob made no effort to conceal his favoritism toward Joseph. When parents try to treat all their children impartially it may be charged by one or more of their children, "Oh, he (or she) is Daddy's, or Mother's pet." But when it is obvious, as it was in Jacob's family, that the special favors shown one child as over against the others are real and not imaginary, this inevitably generates ill will. We are not surprised, therefore, to read that when Joseph's brothers saw unmistakable evidence of their father's favoritism of Joseph, "they hated him, and could not speak peaceably to him."

(4) Apparently the older boys resented Joseph's strict moral standards. Very early in the story we find evidence of this. He was conscientious, dependable, and truthful. Once when he

returned with four of his brothers from pasturing the flocks, his father asked him about the work and conduct of his brothers. He felt impelled to tell the truth even though his brothers were put in an unfavorable light. They considered this an act of disloyalty to them and looked upon him as a tattletale, or, even worse, as his father's spy. Apparently they came to loathe him because he would neither join in nor condone their practices. They looked upon his moral uprightness scornfully as goody-goodyness. This seems to be an ancient instance of one of the strange psychological twists in human personality which emerges now and then in every generation, namely, violently despising someone for no other reason than his honesty and clean moral living.

(5) Joseph was an ambitious lad. Apparently that is what the historian wished to impress upon the readers by relating Joseph's dreams of grandeur. He dreamed, and told about it with relish, that while he was in the field with his brothers, binding the grain into bundles, his bundle stood up straight and his brothers' bundles gathered around and bowed down to his. This was interpreted by him and by his brothers as a sign that some day he would reign over them. "So," adds the writer, "they hated him the more for his dreams and for his words." He had another dream in which the sun, the moon, and eleven stars were bowing down to him. He told this, probably in the same haughty air, to both his brothers and his father. The implication of this dream was so obvious that his father rebuked him, saying, with astonishment, "Shall I and your mother and brothers indeed come to bow ourselves to the ground before you?" The eagerness with which Joseph publicized his dreams was a sign to his perceptive and solicitious father of Joseph's exaggerated opinion of himself, of a heady ambition.

Until this day not too much is known for certain about the causes and significance of dreams. But we would be safe in saying that, at least sometimes, in some unknown way, our night dreams are a reflection in our subconscious minds of our day thoughts. There can be no doubt that Joseph was a capable, perhaps superior, person. He is to be commended for having an ambition to accomplish great things with his abilities, even for feeling that he had a divine destiny, that God had a purpose for his life, or for feeling, as someone put it, "I have a rendezvous with life, that I mean to keep." From the human side we call it ambition; from God's side, destiny. Wise is the person who feels early in his life that he is not here to drift, but to dare and dream and do. But no one, not even a person with the intelligence quotient of a genius, should feel that the possession of abilities and great ambitious gives him the right to strut about, boast of his future achievements, and disdain others with lesser talents and more modest aspirations.

All these things joined together to generate in Joseph's brothers a dangerous mood. Their hatred was likely to turn to violence at the least provocation. That provocation came when their father again *sent* Joseph to check on the boys when they were away from home caring for the flocks. The fact that he was sent, that he had not been with them sharing their labors but was at home in comfort, wearing his special robe, seems to have been what triggered their wrath. When they saw him coming they said to one another, "Here comes the dreamer. Let's kill him and throw him into one of the pits (abandoned cisterns), and then we shall see what will become of his dreams." Reuben, the oldest and supposedly the most mature, who seems to have felt the most responsibility for the young lad, pleaded for his life. He said, "Shed no blood: cast him into this pit here in the wilderness— but lay no hand upon him." As Joseph walked up to the camp the brothers seized him, stripped off the long robe, the very sight of which always aroused their furor, carried him over to the pit, and dumped him in.

Later, while Reuben was away from the camp, the brothers changed their minds and sold Joseph to a group of Ishmaelite traders on their way to Egypt. Their problem now was to agree on what to tell their father. After some discussion they decided to kill a goat, dip Joseph's robe in its blood, show it to their father and let him draw his own conclusion. They said to Jacob, when they returned home, "We found this. See whether you think it is your son's [not "our brother's"] robe or not." When Jacob examined it he cried, "It is my son's robe; a wild beast has devoured him; Joseph is without doubt torn to pieces." If this had happened in our scientific age it could have been discovered, by the proper test, that the blood on the garment was not human blood.

2. Joseph in Egypt.

(1) *A household slave.* Joseph was taken by the traders to the market in Egypt and sold as a domestic slave to a man named Potiphar, who was an official in Pharaoh's government. Joseph was only seventeen years old at the time. He had not yet met the temptations and attractions of his own little world, much less those of a sophisticated society like that of Egypt. He must have been lonely, ill at ease, and handicapped by his inability to speak a foreign language. But he took with him that which enabled him to keep his bearings in that strange, dangerous world: his moral standards, his religious faith, his ideals and dreams. The determining factor in every person's life is not where he is but what he is, not his outward circumstances but his inner convictions.

There is no indication that Joseph railed at his fate, or became embittered over his unjust treatment. Rather, he decided that if he had to be a household slave, he would be as good and as trustworthy a slave as possible. In due time his master recognized his superior qualities and made him overseer of his property and of the personnel of his entire household.

Joseph was a handsome, attractive young fellow. Potiphar's wife became enamored of him and openly invited him to go to bed with her. He said to her frankly, "You are his wife; how then can I do this great wickedness and sin against God?" You see, he had a mystical sense of right. His belief in God obligated him to do the right thing under all circumstances. He was an "inner directed" personality. He had a spiritual radar by which he discovered the honorable thing to do. He had a spiritual gyroscope to keep him in balance. His standards were not determined by statistical polls to discover the guidelines of the majority. He had his own inner, built-in guidelines—his simple, basic principles.

Potiphar's wife refused to take "no" for an answer. One day she became aggressive and grabbed his coat, so that he had to flee from the house leaving his coat in her hands. His master sent him to prison forthwith. Joseph said not a word in his own defense or against the woman. In resisting her Joseph did an uncommon thing. Most men will protect a woman against another man. Some will protect a woman against themselves. Joseph protected a woman against herself.

(2) *A prisoner.* Joseph took his undeserved punishment without acrimony or discouragement. He decided to live by his convictions as a prisoner just as he had as a lad at home and as a domestic slave. His worth was quickly recognized. He was made a trusty. The prisoners and the internal affairs of the prison were placed in his care. A prison was the last place one would expect a man's greatest chance to come to him. But that was exactly what happened to Joseph.

Two of his fellow prisoners were Pharaoh's chief butler and his chief baker, both of whom had offended their master and had been put in prison. Joseph did them a favor by rightly interpreting a disturbing dream for each. The chief baker was ultimately executed but the chief butler was restored to his old position. One night Pharaoh himself had a disturbing dream that neither he nor his magicians and wise men could interpret, whereupon the butler suggested that Joseph, the young Hebrew in prison who had interpreted his dream, might be of assistance to Pharaoh. Joseph was summoned before Pharaoh. He listened to Pharaoh's dream and then interpreted it to mean that there would be seven years of plenty in Egypt to be followed by seven years of famine. He suggested that Pharaoh set up a new Department of Agriculture to prepare for storing grain during the good years to carry them through the bad years of famine. Pharaoh and his advisers agreed that such a wise man should be charged with the responsi-

bility for carrying out the suggested plan and given the authority
to do so.

Pharaoh immediately issued a proclamation making Joseph
second in command over all the land. He took the signet ring
from his finger and put it on Joseph's, arrayed him in royal garments, put a gold chain about his neck, put him in a chariot immediately behind his own, and paraded him through the streets
while the people bowed in obeisance. He gave Joseph an Egyptian
name and gave him for a wife the daughter of the priest of On,
the seat of the worship of the sun god and one of the leading
universities of Egypt for sacred learning.

3. Joseph and his brothers meet again.

(1) *Their first meeting.* By the end of the first seven years of
Joseph's elevation to authority thirteen years had passed since
he left home. He was now thirty years old, the head of a family
and in an important position with the government. During the
next seven years the crops were exceptionally good. These years
were followed by seven years of severe drought not only in Egypt
but in all the countries of the Near East. Egypt was the granary
of that part of the world. Soon groups of people from the sur-
rounding countries began to come to Egypt to buy grain. All who
came for this purpose were required to make application in person
to Joseph.

One day a group of ten men appeared before Joseph, bowing
down their faces to the ground as they begged for the privilege of
purchasing grain. From their features Joseph immediately recognized them as Hebrews and from their clothing, as foreigners.
When he took a second look he was certain they were his ten
brothers who had sold him into slavery. We are told that as soon
as he was sure they were his brothers, the first thing that flashed
into his mind was his early dream of their bowing down before
him that had angered them and for which his father had rebuked
him. That dream had come true before his very eyes. Here was
his chance to get even, to make them "swallow their words," to
give them some of their own medicine. Would he take revenge

on them or not? From here on the story revolves around Joseph's struggle with that question.

Joseph gave no immediate indication that he recognized them. He spoke to them through his Egyptian interpreter, although he could understand what they were saying to each other in Hebrew. He asked them to identify themselves. Although they answered him correctly he treated them roughly. He accused them of being spies. They denied it. This exchange of charges and denials continued for a few moments. Finally Joseph said, "All right, I'll give you a chance to prove you are telling the truth. Let one of you go back home and bring your youngest brother here. The rest of you shall be put in prison until he is brought. If the younger brother fails to come I will know you are spies. Joseph then bluntly ended the interview and ordered them all to be put in prison for three days, presumably so they could do a little private thinking and talking.

After they had "sweated it out" for three days he summoned them to appear before him again. He was in a different mood by this time, for he also had been doing some private thinking. In fact, the record implies that he had been doing something else of prime importance: he had been praying. So he said to them, in essence, "I have another proposal to make. If you will do what I suggest I will let you live. For I fear God." He then proposed that one of their number remain in Egypt, that the rest go back to Canaan with their grain and bring their youngest brother with them on their next trip. They readily agreed to this and chose Simeon to remain.

The brothers began to speak to one another in Hebrew, not knowing that Joseph could understand all they were saying. Among the things he overhead were: "We are guilty concerning our brother. . . . We saw the distress of his soul as he begged for mercy and we would not listen. . . . That's why this distress has come upon us. . . . Didn't I tell you not to sin against the lad? But you wouldn't listen. Now the day of reckoning for his blood has come."

This was too much for Joseph. While they were still talking

he turned away from them to hide his weeping. When he regained his composure he turned toward them and ordered that Simeon be taken to prison, that their sacks be filled with grain, and that they be permitted to return home. Privately, and to quiet his conscience somewhat, at least for a time, he also ordered that after payments for the grain had been made each man's money be put back in his sack and that they be given in addition sufficient provisions for themselves and their donkeys for their return journey.

(2) *Their second meeting.* When the brothers reached home they found their money in their sacks and told their father that this was only one of the strange things that had happened to them. All agreed that these mysterious things foreboded some kind of evil. When the time came for them to return to Egypt for more grain it was with great difficulty that they finally persuaded their father to permit their youngest brother, Benjamin, Joseph's only full brother, now Jacob's favorite son, to accompany them.

By the time they got back to Egypt Joseph had only partially won the battle over his desire for "sweet revenge." He needed further time to determine whether he could be as severe and unyielding with them as they had been with him. Thus far, each time he had tried to hurt them he had succeeded only in hurting himself more. But he also needed time to explore further their state of mind, whether they still hated him, whether they had any real regrets for the way they had treated him. But his first attempt at this was a tame, tender effort. He gave them a formal dinner at the royal palace and brought Simeon out of prison to join them. The brothers watched with amazement and misgivings as the servants seated them according to their ages, beginning with the youngest, who sat nearest Joseph's table. He gave no hint of his identity or of what he was planning further. They all had a merry time together.

After dinner they purchased their grain and made preparations to leave early the next morning. Joseph had already instructed the steward to fill their sacks with as much grain as they could carry, again to put each man's money in his sack, and to hide his special silver divining cup in Benjamin's sack. Shortly after they left the next morning Joseph sent an officer in pursuit, with orders to overtake them and charge them with stealing his cup. They denied having taken it and encouraged the officer to search all the sacks. They were dumfounded when the cup was found in Benjamin's sack. They were taken back and brought before Joseph. He chastised them sternly and announced that he had decided to keep Benjamin as his personal slave and to let the others go. Judah made a courageous and eloquent plea for Benjamin's release, not for his sake, but for the sake of his aged father in Canaan. His plea was more than Joseph could endure. He could not control himself and made no effort to do so. He broke down unashamedly in the presence of all who were in the room. When he could speak he asked everybody else to withdraw and leave him alone with the men. When he had quieted himself he made himself known to them. They could not believe him, and were a long time responding to his approaches. Finally they were convinced that he was their brother, but they still responded indifferently.

Then, as if he were afraid they might speak and condemn themselves, he urged them not to be angry with themselves, but to accept this turn of events as the providence of God, as God's divine means of preserving their lives and the lives of all the members of their tribe through the remaining years of the drought. The last thing he said to them before they left was, "Do not quarrel on the way," as if to say, "Do not try to lay the blame each on the other and thus relive the past. Rather, let us thank God and move into the future again as one family." They returned home, brought Jacob and their relatives and possessions to Egypt, and settled in a choice section of the land. The tribe remained there not five years, as planned, but four hundred years, or until the time of Moses.

III

The genius of this story is this: In a day when the customs of the times would not have condemned him if he had slain his brothers before his eyes, or permitted them to starve to death, Joseph could not permit himself to take this way out. At no time while he was making himself known to them and demonstrating that he had forgiven them did they tell him they were sorry for mistreating him, or ask him for forgiveness. In fact, despite the fact that on his dying bed Jacob exacted a promise from them that they would ask Joseph's forgiveness, they did not do so.

Joseph's magnanimity demonstrated itself in that he forgave before he was forgiven. His forgiveness was not contingent upon his brothers! He did not wait for them to purge their souls but first purged his own. He practiced the gospel of forgiveness fifteen hundred years or more before Christ gave it to the world. That constitutes the wonder and the supreme worth of this story.

At the beginning I said that Joseph was a conspicuous example of the responsible person. Components of this responsibleness were: he felt he was divinely destined to great and noble things; he had a mystical sense of right; he was undaunted by misfortune; he was too big, too wise, to nurse bitter feelings. All these things were the fruits of his profound belief that all of life should be lived under the consciousness of God. His faith in God enabled him to stand the strains and stresses of life, to triumph over its sorrows, to overcome its temptations, to purge his soul of ugly moods, to find power for living by his ideals. In short, his reasons and his resources for living were rooted in his religious faith.

A medical doctor once remarked that faith is a biological necessity. By this he meant that belief in God is essential to a healthful functioning of one's body. He could just as truly have added that it is also a psychological necessity and a social necessity, because it contributes to a wholesome functioning of one's emotions and to his wholesome functioning as a member of society.

We sometimes hear the question asked, "What is there in religion?" The story of Joseph is a suitable place to find answers to that question, for Joseph exemplifies what religion is all about, what it should mean and can mean to a person's successful living.

THE GREAT, GOOD, GLAD NEWS

... *"Be not afraid; for behold, I bring you good news of a great joy
which will come to all the people; for to you is born this day in the
city of David a Savior, who is Christ the Lord. . . ." And suddenly
there was with the angel a multitude of the heavenly host praising
God and saying, "Glory to God in the highest, and on earth peace
among men with whom he is pleased!"*

—LUKE 2:10-14

I

SOME YEARS AGO, on the Sunday before Christmas, while
the congregation was leaving the sanctuary, the wife of one
of the elders of the church handed me a piece of stationery on
which she had typed these lines:

> From the tumult and the hurry,
> From the tissue and the string,
> From the dollars that are spent on mounds of stuff;
> From the brow with lines of worry
> O'er some petty, petty thing;
> From the tired feet that cannot rush enough;
> From the phrase superlative
> O'er some trifle that we give;
> From the hubbub I would rise and go afar.
> I would seek a quiet place
> Where I could exult in space,
> And my eyes could strain ahead and see a star.

—TERA LEE WAGNER

117

She was the mother of several children. Her family was accustomed to the buying, the wrapping, and the exchange of gifts, a beautifully decorated Christmas tree, "stockings hung by the chimney with care" to be filled by Santa Claus, the singing and playing of Christmas carols and songs, and a sumptuous Christmas dinner. She was not discounting the values of all these things, nor recommending their discontinuance. To her, and to most of us, I dare say, Christmases in our homes are among the most blessed memories of our childhood and will be also to our children, and, we hope, to our grandchildren.

But she was voicing a feeling that most of us have experienced now and then, namely, that it is possible to engage in and to be thrilled by all the things customarily associated with Christmas and still miss the full-orbed meaning of Christ's coming into the world as it was heralded by the angels in Bethlehem. She craved *that* for herself and for her family. She wanted to hear *that* proclaimed by preacher and people to all mankind throughout the world.

Christmas is not just another holiday, not the reproduction in dramatic form of the story of a mother and her baby in the manger, the visit of the shepherds and later of the wise men; nor the retelling of customs and legends, such as St. Nicholas and Santa Claus and his reindeers and the lighting of the Yule Log, that have sprung up around the ancient stories; nor the display of art inspired by the Madonna and child; nor the singing of sacred carols and popular songs, including "Jingle Bells" and "Rudolph, the Red-nosed Reindeer" and all the rest.

Christmas is not a cult that has grown up around the baby Jesus. The baby Jesus was but the beginning—the birth—of the Gospel. The baby grew into manhood. He became a teacher and preacher who spoke immortal truths. He died on a cross for the sins of mankind. He was buried and arose from the dead. He returned in the person and power of the Holy Spirit to be the constant companion, comforter, and friend of man. He established a Church to become his instrument in the world for the proclamation and the practice of his Gospel through the ages, to the bounds of the earth, and to the end of time. It takes all of these things together to constitute the good news of Christmas.

What, then, is the great, good, glad news we celebrate and re-announce at this blessed season? Let us try to find suitable answers to that question by examining the *entire* New Testament. Let's endeavor to discover what that Testament tells us about the grownup teacher, the crucified, buried, resurrected Redeemer and the ever-present life-giving Spirit we call our Lord. Only in this larger setting can we understand the full significance of Christ's birth.

To begin with and as a background for what follows, let me trace the word "new" and the expression "in Christ" through the New Testament. Here are a few of the uses of the word "new": new testament, new covenant, new creature, new man, new earth, and John's picture in bold, daring symbols in the Book of Revelation of a new heaven and a new earth, and of Christ sitting upon the throne saying, "Behold! I make *all* things new."

The expression "in Christ" or its equivalent was used to explain nearly everything the early Christians did and dreamed of. God was "in Christ" (II Cor. 5:19). Nothing will be able to separate us from the love of God "in Christ" (Rom. 8:39). Our bodies are members "of Christ" (I Cor. 6:15). If any man is "in Christ" he is a new creation (II Cor. 5:17). God's plan is to unite all things in heaven and on earth "in him" [Christ] (Eph. 1:10). We are his workmanship created "in Christ" Jesus for good works (Eph. 2:10). God will supply every need of ours according to his riches "in Christ" Jesus (Phil. 4:19). Paul said he could do all things "in Christ" who strengthened him (Phil. 4:13). We have the fullness of life "in Christ" (Col. 2:9). Our life is hid "with Christ" in God (Col. 3:3).

In the light of these and other passages that could be quoted, I believe we are justified in saying that Christ's birth brought good news about God in Christ, about Man in Christ, about Life in Christ, and about the World in Christ.

II

1. Christmas is good news about a new (conception of) God in Christ.

". . . His name shall be called Emmanuel (which means, God with us)" (Matt. 1:23). "He who has seen me has seen the Father" (John 14:9). "God was in Christ reconciling the world unto himself" (II Cor. 5:19). "In him the whole fulness of deity dwells bodily" (Col. 2:9).

Thus the New Testament says in no uncertain terms that in Christ God revealed himself—his nature or character, his personality, if you wish, his purposes, his hopes for the human race. Or, as some state it, "God is a living Christ," or, "God *is* what Christ was." If we want to know who and what God is, what he wants and expects of us, take a good look at Christ.

We can break those generalities down into a few specifics and say that the New Testament reveals that (1) *God is real, or alive.* That school of theologians who call themselves followers of Christ and students of the New Testament and yet say that God is dead, could not be farther from the truth. They are, in fact, dealing irresponsibly with the Scriptures about which they profess to be talking. God's existence, or reality, or aliveness, is assumed in the New Testament from beginning to end. That assumption underlies everything Christ said and did and everything that the writers of the New Testament said about him.

Next, the New Testament reveals that (2) *God is actively in charge of the universe.* Christ said this or implied it continuously. When Paul quoted a line from a Greek poem, "In Him we live and move and have our being," he was expressing a belief that is basic to Christ and to all the early Christians—that this universe was originated and is sustained, supervised, and operated by God.

Again, the New Testament reveals that (3) *God is a person.* The New Testament—the entire Bible as for that—pictures God as having qualities we associate only with persons. Jesus called God our "heavenly Father," and pictured Him as doing things for His children that earthly fathers do for theirs. He is described as thinking, speaking, and feeling, as being moved by emotions, notably love, that characterize human beings. He forgives. He suffers. In fact, the death of Christ is spoken of as the suffering, forgiving love of God for the redemption of His children.

Still again, the New Testament reveals that (4) *God and man can have fellowship with one another*. They can converse in prayer. The Divine and human minds can meet, their hearts can beat together, their personalities can touch. And this "fellowship of kindred minds" has immeasurable results for the inner life of man.

Now, all this is good news about God. Always it is good news to all men under all circumstances and in all situations. It is great, glad news to be assured that God is real, alive, in charge of the universe and all its forces; to be told that God did not wind up the universe like a machine and leave it to run itself thereafter; that He did not exhaust Himself in its creation, but is still at work; that we are not orphans, left to the whims and fancies of the forces that play around us, mere victims of those forces. It is good news to hear that God is our Father, our friend, our companion; that He loves us with a never-failing, forgiving, redeeming love; that He is involved in everything we do, identified with us, our ever-present, daily helper. Believe that! Live as though it is true and every day will be Christmas.

2. Christmas is good news about new men in Christ.

The central fact on which our Christian doctrine of man is based is that God entered into human life in Christ, that He became a human being in all the meanings of that term. "The Word of God became flesh and dwelt among us" (John 1:14). Jesus became a real man subjected Himself to all the experiences common to human beings. That very act emphasizes the high value God puts on the being He has created. It ennobles, elevates, dignifies him. "See what love the Father has given us, that we should be called children of God; and so we are," here and now (I John 3:1). In effect, God is saying to human beings what the prophet said to his debased, discouraged people of old,

"Arise, shine; for your light has come, and the glory of the Lord has risen upon you" (Isaiah 60:1).

The Old Testament creation story says that man was made in the image and after the likeness of God. The Christmas story tells us that God has taken upon Himself the image and likeness of man. So God is like us! We no longer hesitate to think of God in human terms and do not hesitate also to feel that there is something God-like, something divine in us, at least potentially. But that is not all. The gospel goes on to say that man can be born again, created anew, by the Spirit of God, and enabled to achieve in some degree the qualities of God. "If any one is in Christ, he is a new creation; the old has passed away, behold, the new has come" (II Cor. 5:17). We are exhorted, therefore to "put on the new nature, created after the likeness of God" (Eph. 4:24). We are reminded that our life is "hid with Christ in God" (Col. 3:3) and exhorted to "put off the old nature with its practices and put on the new nature, which is being renewed in knowledge after the image of its creator," and to "put on as God's chosen ones" all the Christian graces described in the writings of the apostles.

All this is good news, challenging news. We get discouraged about ourselves and about the whole human race, and not without reasons. But when we remember who we are, and who we can become with the renewing and regenerating power of God's love and grace and spiritual presence, we look up and "press on toward the goal for the prize of the upward call of God in Christ Jesus" (Phil. 3:14).

> O holy Child of Bethlehem,
> Descend on us, we pray;
> Cast out our sin and enter in,
> Be born in us today.
> We hear the Christmas angels,
> The great glad tidings tell;
> O come to us, abide with us,
> Our Lord, Emmanuel.
> PHILLIPS BROOKS

3. Christmas is good news about new life in Christ.

"I came that they may have life and have it abundantly" (John 10:10). "Whoever drinks of the water that I shall give him will never thirst; the water that I shall give him will become in him a spring of water welling up to eternal life" (John 4:14). And remember that when John speaks of eternal life he is speaking of something we experience here and now in this world, in these fleshy bodies, this material world, where we "labor and are heavy laden," where we marry and build homes and try to build civilizations, and mourn and suffer. God is with us in the common ways of life. An old hymn we used to sing, and that I wish we still sang occasionally, says that

> Celestial fruits on earthly ground
> From faith and hope may grow.

> The hill of Zion yields
> A thousand sacred sweets,
> Before we reach the heavenly fields,
> Or walk the golden streets.

> We're marching through Immanuel's ground
> To fairer worlds on high.

ISAAC WATTS

The "peace of God which passes all understanding," the "joy unspeakable and full of glory," the "abundant life in Christ," all the "fruits of the Spirit," may be ours now, in the experiences of our common human life.

It is good news to know that this is as life should be and can be to Christians. If at just one Christmas season—this one—we could attain an all-inclusive understanding of what the birth of Christ really means to our human race, the joys of the season can carry over into all the practical affairs of daily life throughout the year. And thus we can come to know from personal experience what Paul meant by a "life hid with Christ in God" (Col. 3:3).

Charles Dickens' *A Christmas Carol* has lived and thrilled and made its way into the hearts of many generations primarily for one reason: that it glorifies the home—the Christmas dinner, the festive games, the simple worship, the joys and the sorrows—of one ordinary family, the Cratchett family.

> It isn't far to Bethlehem town,
> It's anywhere that Christ comes down
> And finds in people's friendly face,
> A welcome and abiding place.
> The road to Bethelehem runs right through
> The homes of folks like me and you.

4. Christmas is good news about a new world in Christ.

"God so loved the *world* that he gave his only son" (John 3:16). "I bring you good news of a great joy which will come to *all the people*" (Luke 2:11) . . . "And there was a multitude of the heavenly host praising God and saying, "Glory to God in the highest and on earth peace among men with whom he is pleased" (Luke 2:13, 14). Peace can come only through men with whom God is well pleased. It was to begin with, it is now, and it always will be the function of the church of God to be the instrument of God for producing such men. The dream of peace on earth is one of the oldest dreams of mankind. It is part and parcel of the gospel. Only men of good will can guarantee that peace and nothing but the regenerating power of the Spirit of God can produce such men.

One of the oldest documents extant (c. A.D. 100) is a letter written by an unknown person to another person addressed as Diognetus. In this letter the writer, among other things said: "What the soul is to the body, that Christians are to the world. The soul is dispersed through all the members of the body, and Christians are scattered through all the cities of the world." The implication is that already, as early as A.D. 100, newborn Christians were pouring new life into the society in which they lived and labored. A modern way of saying the same thing as the ancient letter, would be, "Christians are the bloodstream of society. Just as the blood circulates through the body, giving life to every cell of it, so Christians do—or ought to do—in their world, their social order where "they live and move and have their being."

It is good news that Christ came into the world to make such men for such a task and good news that God's Spirit can still make such men, if they will give Him a chance. That, my friends, is the hope of the world—the hope of a peaceful, brotherly world.

III

Bret Harte has a story of how a baby came to Roaring Mine Camp and changed it that is symbolic of what the coming of Christ into the world has meant to some extent and can continue to mean until this old world is transformed into God's kingdom.

A poor woman with a questionable reputation, the only woman in the whole of the camp, died. She left behind a small baby and the men of the camp had to take care of it. The baby was lying in a box. The men felt that a box was not fit for a baby's crib. So they sent one of their members eighty miles on a mule to Sacramento to get a rosewood cradle. When the cradle came the rags on which the baby was sleeping seemed out of place. So the man was sent back to Sacramento to purchase some clothes—lacy, frilly clothes. When the baby was dressed in its lovely garments and placed in the rosewood cradle, the men observed for the first time that the floor was dirty. So they scrubbed it clean. Then they noticed that the walls and ceiling were also dirty. So they scrubbed them. Then they noticed that the walls and ceiling were unsightly. So they proceeded to whitewash them. Afterward they mended the windows and draped them. And because the baby needed to be quiet at times, they remained still and ceased some of their rough language and rowdy ways. When the weather permitted they took the cradle out to the mines and discovered that the mining area had to be cleaned and flowers planted to make the surroundings as lovely and as attractive as the baby. Finally the men began to improve their personal appearances. Thus the coming of a baby resulted in the transformation of Roaring Mine Camp into a new and attractive place.

In like manner the birth of Jesus and the gospel that grew out of that event can make men new, give us new life and transform our world into a place fit for the abode of our Lord, *if* enough of us will offer ourselves as God's instruments for this task.

The best way for each of us to celebrate Christmas this year is to say afresh to God, "I believe that good news. I propose to act upon it. Begin your divine process of transformation right now with me."

I shall not hear the angels sing
    As long ago they sang;
I shall not hear their trumpets ring
    As long ago they rang;
But silently as snowflakes fall
    Into the silent sea,
The Lord of angels and of all,
    Will come this day to me!

The star I shall not see with awe
    That blazed when He was born,
Nor see Him as the angels saw
    On that first Christmas morn;
But He will come, divinely fair,
    Love-lighted and love-led,
My heart the lowly manger where
    He deigns to lay His head.

I shall not hear the angels sing
    As when at first He came;
Celestial trumpets will not ring
    The music of His name;

No signs and wonders as of old
This day will set apart,
But what more wondrous than to hold
The Word within my heart!"

—"My Christmas Guest"
DENIS A. McCARTHY

WHAT'S GOOD ABOUT GOOD FRIDAY?

When Jesus had received the vinegar, he said, "It is finished"; and he bowed his head and gave up his spirit.

—JOHN 19:30

I

TRADITIONALLY Good Friday has been observed as a sad, dark day, a day of tragedy. In the Roman Catholic church the priests and attendants are vested in black, the altar is stripped of its ornaments, and the day is turned into a day of mourning. Recently in a sermon in *The Pulpit*, a national journal for preachers, I came across an extreme statement of this point of view by a Protestant preacher. He said, "The expression 'Good Friday' is unfortunate and misleading. Since when is an execution or a funeral a good thing? . . . The term 'Black Friday,' remains the accurate and necessary one." If that is all that today means, why did Christians ever call it *Good* Friday?

There is no available information to indicate when the custom of calling it Good Friday arose. Some have speculated that originally it was called "God's Friday," and that later through some mistake or corruption of words it became "Good" Friday. That the day was a sad, bleak day for the followers of the Master is clearly indicated in the New Testament records. But that the early Christians quickly began to think of it not merely as a tragic day that called for mourning, but as a significant day

128

that called for rejoicing and thanksgiving, is also clearly indicated in the same records. Christians have valid reasons for calling it a good day.

So I wish to raise, and try to find answers to the question, "What's good about Good Friday?"

Since the services on Good Friday are often devoted to the seven words of Jesus on the Cross, an appropriate place to begin the search for our answer is the last words He uttered just before He died, "It is finished."

II

1. What did Jesus mean by that expression?

(1) Conceivably He might have meant that this was the end of His earthly trials, including His physical agony. According to all the information we have crucifixion was an excruciating experience. "It is finished" could have meant that His suffering was over. Just as we sometimes say of a person who dies after undergoing long suffering from an extended illness, "Thank God, his terrible agonies are over," Jesus might have himself said, "I'm glad it is all over at last." Many years ago a British physician wrote a book entitled *The Physical Cause of the Death of Christ*. His chief interest was in the statement found in John's Gospel, that when they came to break the legs of the three men to hasten their death, they found Jesus already dead. Whereupon one of the soldiers pierced the side of Jesus with his spear and "at once there came out blood and water." From certain physiological information available to him as a scientist this physician concluded from the fact that blood and water came out so quickly after Jesus' death that He had died not from the physical effects of crucifixion but from a psychological condition such as a broken heart. Jesus did have many experiences sufficient to break His heart. Not the least of these was that He was opposed by His countrymen, by His friends, and even by His own relatives. But His cry, "It is finished," had a much more significant meaning than, "Well, my troubles are now over."

(2) Or—and this is more likely—He could have meant that He had finished His divine mission on earth. Significantly enough John puts it this way, "After this, Jesus knowing that all was now finished, said 'I thirst' and then a moment or two later, 'It is finished.' " The linguists tell us that the Greek word translated "finished" also means "achieved" or "accomplished." Some scholars, therefore, insist that His cry, "It is finished," was not a sigh of relief but a shout of triumph. The Apostle John reports that in His long prayer (John 17:4) Jesus said, "I glorified Thee on earth, having accomplished the work which thou gavest me to do." Well, exactly what was that work?

(a) He had fulfilled his ministry as a teacher of the ideals and principles of the good life, the happy, blessed, successful human life. As important as that was, it was but one aspect of His ministry.

(b) He also had fulfilled His function as a prophet of God, proclaiming the ideals of a divine society on earth, which He called "the Kingdom of God." I think it was James Russell Lowell who once said that there is enough dynamite in the gospel of Jesus to blow our social institutions to pieces. And, of course, there is, if His ideals of justice, mercy, and love were to be put rapidly into practice in our human relationships.

Apparently many of His followers believed this to be His major purpose. Some of His supporters were what we now call "Zealots," who, to the very end, expected Him to start a social, or even a political revolution. After the feeding of the 5,000 some of the people physically tried to declare Him their earthly king. But when He "perceived" what they were about to do, He expressed his opposition to such a procedure by turning His back upon the crowd and withdrawing "into the hills by himself" (John 6:15). When He made what we call His triumphal entry into Jerusalem on Palm Sunday a group of His followers interpreted this to mean He was publicly declaring Himself to be their Messiah-King. In fact, Peter, moved by this mistaken notion, drew his sword and began to use it to try to kill Jesus' enemies when they arrested Him in the garden of Gethsemane. For this Jesus took Peter severely to task and told him to put up his sword. This was equivalent to saying that Peter and those of like mind completely misunderstood the kind of kingdom about which He had been preaching. Some of His intimate disciples, members of His inner circle, admitted after the Crucifixion that they were disappointed because they had "thought he was the one to redeem Israel," that is, to restore her to her ancient earthly glory (Lk. 24:21). Pilate was actually frightened at the possibility of Jesus' trying to lead a Jewish political movement to declare their independence of Rome.

But at the outset of His public ministry Jesus decided not to be a social revolutionist. During His temptation in the wilderness He rejected that as a possible method of achieving His goals. In His early ministry, He also contrasted His own method with the method of John the Baptist to take the Kingdom of God by force (Matt. 11:11f) and rejected it. As I understand the Four Gospels they tell us specifically that the purpose of Jesus was not primarily to win followers and train them how to mobilize and utilize their combined economic, political, military, and organizational resources to bring the Kingdom of God by sheer force. Throughout His ministry He spoke only of the use of spiritual force toward that end. He definitely chose not to be a social revolutionist.

(c) He had finished a notable ministry of humanitarianism—of healing the sick, feeding the hungry, caring for the needy and oppressed. In his address during his early evangelistic campaign before the household of Cornelius, Peter spoke of Jesus as a man who "went about doing good." One of the poems of John Greenleaf Whittier, now set to music as a hymn, exhorts us to "follow with reverent steps the great example of him whose holy work was doing good." But I beseech you to find time during the Easter season to read the Gospel of Mark hurriedly with only one purpose in view: to discover the many times—twelve times to be exact—in his brief book where Mark specifically stated that Jesus tried to avoid doing good. At times He strictly "ordered them," those whom He healed and those who witnessed it, not to publicize these healings. At times He traveled incognito to prevent being identified. Once, after healing a man, and to avoid attracting large crowds He "charged" him—literally shook His finger at him—as He said, "Go straight home, through the open fields, not through the villages; do not tell anyone of your healing." At least once He used a ruse to outwit the crowd and get away from them. Once He took the crowds to task for following Him merely to get food, not to hear the words of the gospel.

Why all this effort to avoid merely helping people? Unquestionably this was for the purpose of finding time to fulfill another purpose, another function, another mission of greater importance to mankind. What was that more important mission? When we have found the correct answer to that question we will have found the key to the proper understanding of his Crucifixion.

(d) There is one more thing that emerges from the pages of the New Testament, as clearly as daylight, and that is this: When Jesus cried, "It is finished," He had completed His work as the Redeemer of mankind. This redemptive mission on earth was intimately bound up with His death. We are told that Joseph, in a dream before the birth of Jesus, was instructed to give the boy the name "Jesus," which means "savior," and that this was in order to fulfill the ancient prophecy of the birth of one whose name would be called "Emmanuel," meaning "God with us." The two great truths—"Savior" and "God with us"—merged in the Cross. In His death God revealed Himself to be the God of redemptive love.

Several times during His ministry Jesus tried to prepare His followers for His coming death. Once on the way to Jerusalem He told them that He would suffer many things and be killed, whereupon Peter rebuked Him saying, "God forbid, Lord. This shall never happen to you." Jesus in turn rebuked Peter, saying, "Get behind me, Satan! You are a hindrance to me, for you are not on the side of God but of men!" This amounted to saying, "You simply are not thinking about my mission as God is. You do not understand what God is doing through my suffering." On the Cross he prayed, "Father, forgive them, for they

know not what they do," as if to say, "They do not understand—
cannot understand yet—what you are doing today. They think
only that they are killing me, a despised criminal. The significance of what you are doing for them or saying to them through
my death is as yet hidden from them." In short, He tried to
explain His suffering to them. But they simply were not prepared
to understand it. So we must turn to the Epistles of the New
Testament to discover what the early Christians thought about
the Cross.

2. What did the death of Jesus mean to the early Church?

As we have seen, His followers at first were crushed. Their
hopes were blighted. Then after they were convinced of His
resurrection and living presence—after they had thought through
all that He had said to them about going into the world and
preaching the gospel—they began to interpret His death as the
crowning act of His earthly mission. When that happened they
began to think of it as a cosmic event: God's act of redemption
for the entire human race.

The Apostle Paul set forth this idea in its largest terms in a
daring passage in the 8th chapter of his letter to the Romans:
He wrote, "The sufferings of this present time are not worth
comparing with the glory that is to be revealed to us. For the
creation waits with eager longing for the revealing of the sons
of God. . . . We know that the whole creation has been groaning
in travail together until now; and not only the creation but we
ourselves, who have the first fruits of the Spirit, groan inwardly
as we wait for adoption as sons . . ." (8:18-19, 22-23).

Let us try to understand what Paul means by these statements.
What he is saying is that "all creation is involved in the fortunes
of humanity," that the universe is "a basis and framework for
the immense spiritual adventure"—God's spiritual adventure—
with the human race. That adventure began in the mind of God
when He started the universe on its way. All the outlay of energy,
all the struggle and agonizing effort from the creation of man
until Christ, may be thought of as birth pangs to bring forth

fullgrown sons of God. The climax of God's suffering toward this end was His redemptive love in the death of Christ. Man's redemption in Christ was that "one far-off, divine event toward which the whole creation moved." This is the only setting, as difficult as it is to grasp, in which we can properly understand the significance of the Cross.

The effort to explain this amazing event is the central purpose of the New Testament writers. We shall never grasp the full meaning of the Cross until we believe and make our own what those early Christians declared unceasingly, namely, that the Cross was God's disclosure of His nature and character—of the kind of Being He always has been and always will be. We read, for example, "God was in Christ reconciling the world unto himself" (II Cor. 3:16); "In him the whole fullness of deity dwells bodily" (Col. 2:9); "He reflects the glory of God and bears the very stamp of his nature" (Heb. 1:3). "He who has seen me," said the Master, "has seen the Father" (John 14:9). Or, as Paul expressed it, "The whole creation groaneth and travaileth in pain until now, awaiting the arrival of the sons of God."

All the efforts, the struggles, of God for and with the human race since its creation, had one purpose in view: to aid us in becoming His children, in growing into His likeness. That effort has cost Him continuous sufferings. Through the suffering of Christ on the Cross we get a new glimpse into the very heart of God. He is—eternally is—a suffering God. God is involved deeply, inextricably, with us. He cannot leave us to fight alone. "If God dieth not for man and giveth not himself eternally for man, man could not exist." Someone once said that if he were God and man made such a mess of things with his war, hatred, murder, lust, cobwebs of infamy, etc., he would "sweep him to one side and start anew." Then with a start the thought struck him, "But if I did this would I be God?" The answer that comes from the Cross is, "If he did that he would not be God."

But what if He [Jesus] came to the earth to show
By the path of pain that he trod

The blistering flame of eternal shame
That burns in the heart of God?

G. STUDDERT-KENNEDY

That is exactly what the New Testament tells us Christ came to show. Over and over we are told such things as these: "God commendeth his love toward us, in that, while we were yet sinners, Christ died for us" (Rom. 5:8); "At the right time Christ died for the ungodly" (Rom. 5:6); "Christ died for sins once for all" (I Pet. 3:18); "By this we know love, that he laid down his life for us" (I John 3:16); "Not that we loved God but that he loved us and sent his son to be the expiation for our sins" (I John 4:10). In a small Italian church there is a painting which at first glance is only another picture of the Crucifixion. But a second look shows it to be different. Back of the figure of Christ can be seen a shadowy figure of God Himself. The nail that pierces the hand of Jesus goes through the hand of God. The spear thrust into the side of Jesus goes through God's side. The artist who painted that picture was trying to say in his own way what the New Testament says, that we do not begin to fathom the depths of meaning in the Cross until we take it as a revelation of God's eternal suffering for the redemption of all who will accept Him.

The Cross is not an ancient event only. It is also a present fact. It reveals not merely what God was but what He is. He is a suffering, forgiving, loving, redeeming God. The death of Christ did not make God willing to love us and save us. It revealed that He is always willing to do so. That did not make redemption possible. It made it fully and finally known. It did not placate a tyrant God who was waiting to punish His children. It reassured men that God is not hostile toward them: that regardless of— in spite of—their sins, He stands ready to forgive. It did not cause God to love the world, but told us that God has always loved the world, that is to say, Jesus, in his life, ministry, death, and resurrection, revealed to us the character of God as He is here and now.

3. What does or can the death of Jesus mean to us?

Now we are ready to answer our question: "What's good about Good Friday?" The answer is simple, yet profound. Speaking first in general terms, in commemorating the death of Jesus we are commemorating the unveiling of the eternal heart of God—the disclosure of His divine nature. Nothing can separate us from Him. Under all conditions that human beings face we can call Him "Emmanuel," God with us. He understands our problems and needs and makes them His own. So, there is no such thing as a hopeless situation with God. There is always light ahead. The Apostle Paul stated this in one of his famous, immortal passages in the 8th chapter of Romans that concludes, "I am sure that neither death, nor life, nor angels, nor principalities, nor things present, nor things to come, nor powers, nor height, nor depth, nor anything else in all creation, will be able to separate us from the love of God in Christ Jesus our Lord" (Romans 8:38-39).

Speaking now specifically, here are the good things about Good Friday. (1) God is with us, as we go through the strains, stresses, and struggles of living. God planned this universe. Just living involves hardships and efforts. Just why He planned it thus we cannot know for certain. But we know that this is our Father's world, and we are His offspring. He knows the way we have to take, the inevitable struggle of life. We can therefore be sure that He will never let us down. "O Love that wilt not let me go, I rest my weary soul in Thee . . ."; "We bear the strain of earthly care, but bear it not alone; beside us walks our Brother Christ and makes our task his own." The burden is heavy. The yoke is not easy. But we are assured of our divine "Yoke-fellow."

(2) God is with us in our sorrows. Again, the sufferings that seem to be built in—somehow part and parcel of life itself—are mysteries. But we are not left to endure them alone. They will not go to waste. They must have meaning beyond our ability to fathom. God is enduring them with us: so we will not lose heart.

When the woes of life o'ertake me,
    Hopes deceive, and fears annoy,
Never shall the cross forsake me:
    Lo! it glows with peace and joy.

Bane and blessing, pain and pleasure,
    By the cross are sanctified;
Peace is there that knows no measure,
    Joys that through all time abide.

                              JOHN BOWRING

(3) God is with us in our sins. Even sin cannot separate us from Him. He understands the problems we have of living with ourselves and with our fellowmen. He struggles with us when we are struggling with our temptations and sins and wrongs. There is always forgiveness, always another chance, always the possibility of redemption and a better day. The death of Christ at the outset was regarded by the first Christians as the agony through which God Himself goes because of our sins, His heart longing and yearning to forgive. Again that was not an ancient, but is a present, event: God suffers with us and for us in our sins now. I don't know of anyone who has put this truth into more dramatic, appealing words than John Masefield in "The Everlasting Mercy." A young Quaker woman who worked among the derelicts at night in London entered a saloon where Saul Kane, half drunk, was threatening violence and spewing out profanity as he waved his half empty glass of liquor. At a dramatic moment the young woman walked up to him, took his glass from his hands, emptied it on the sawdust floor, and said,

> Saul Kane, when next you drink,
> Do me the gentleness to think,
> That every drop of drink accursed,
> Makes Christ within you die of thirst;
> That every dirty word you say,
> Is one more flint upon His way,

Another thorn about His head,
Another mock by where He tread,
Another nail, another cross.
All that you are is that Christ's loss.

III

Yes, this can be a good Good Friday for you, if you will only choose to make it so. There is only one appropriate response to the Cross of Christ: "Love so amazing, so divine, demands my life, my soul, my all."

We may not know, we cannot tell,
What pains he had to bear;
But we believe it was for us,
He hung and suffered there.

O dearly, dearly has He loved,
And we must love him, too.
And trust in His redeeming blood,
And try His works to do.
Cecil Frances Alexander

I do not pretend to be able to explain all this neatly to my own satisfaction, much less to the satisfaction of all types of human minds, including the theologians of all schools. But I believe it. It is one of my most precious Christian beliefs. "Lord, I believe; help thou my unbelief" (Mark 9:24).